AN ILLUSTRATED HISTORY C
BOOKS IN THE CHAINED LIBF
WELLS CATHEDRAL, SOMERSET

BY KEVIN SPEARS

FOR HELENA AND CECILIA

STAINED GLASS WINDOW OF THE
ARMS OF BISHOP BUBWITH, WHO
GAVE THE MONEY TO BUILD THE
LIBRARY IN HIS WILL OF 1424 🍃

AN
ILLUSTRATED HISTORY
OF THE BOOKS IN THE
CHAINED LIBRARY
OF
WELLS
CATHEDRAL
SOMERSET

BY

KEVIN SPEARS

❧ ❧ ❧

🐚

CECHEL

This book was first printed by ST. ANDREW'S PRESS OF WELLS,
SOMERSET *for* CECHEL BOOKS, *in an edition of* TWO HUNDRED *copies.*

· DECEMBER MMXVI ·

ISBN 978-1-5262-0657-2
A CIP catalogue record for this book is available from the British Library.

Text styling, design and artwork by
Bernard Chandler, Glastonbury, England.
www.graffik.co.uk

Text set in Plantin 11.5pt on 16pt,
with Univers Condensed 10pt,
Centaur titling and Jenson.

Printed and bound in Great Britain by St. Andrew's Press, Wells, Somerset
MMXVI, MMXVII

CONTENTS

ACKNOWLEDGEMENTS

THE INSPIRATION FOR THIS BOOK came from the talented and dedicated team of fifty volunteers who keep the library at Wells cathedral open throughout the year and field questions from the 16,000 visitors who come to see it. Many of them have played a part in this book's production. Most notable is Jim Woodcock who took all the photographs of the library and its books. Without his abilities and willingness to give so many hours of support in not just taking the photographs but editing them for publication, this book would not have been started. I owe him a great debt of gratitude.

I am also grateful to many other library volunteers for their active support, especially Alastair Barr, Anne Crawford, John Cryer and Rose Sanguinetti who read through initial draft chapters and encouraged me to keep writing.

Professor Ian Gadd at Bath Spa University found the time to look through an early draft. He very sensibly advised me that I needed an extra chapter on the title page, and sent me material to assist. I am very honoured that such an eminent scholar in the field of the history of the book offered to write a generous foreword.

And my thanks to Dr. Julia Wood, Wells City Archivist, for researching early booksellers in the city. And at the final stages, my thanks to Bill Welland for sharing his experience of self-publishing.

I am grateful to the Chapter of Wells cathedral and to the Rector of Bath Abbey for waiving the normal fees for reproducing photographs of their books held in the Chained Library.

I would also like to thank Bernard Chandler for turning my draft into what is a very professional looking book, and to Tim Wood at St. Andrew's Press in Wells for his advice and for managing the printing process.

My thanks also to my wife, Lindsey, for her encouragement and her forbearance as more and more books on the history of books and libraries arrived in the post to aid my research.

All other photographs and illustrations were taken wherever possible from the Creative Commons website (https://creativecommons.org/) to avoid copyright issues. Where this was not possible, illustrations have been acknowledged and links to websites given. In some cases permission has been generously given to reproduce the illustrations. If, despite my best efforts, any illustrations have not been properly acknowledged, I can only apologise and guarantee that the omission will be corrected in any future revision.

FOREWORD

THE 'HISTORY OF THE BOOK' is a field of study that pays close attention to the physical form that a written text takes, whether it is a manuscript, a printed book, or even an electronic text. It sees a book not as something created solely by an author but as the tangible product of a series of intellectual, artistic, and commercial decisions taken by one or more individuals, often highly skilled. We are well used to the idea of a library as an important repository of human knowledge, but libraries also give us privileged insights into the ways in which societies have, over the centuries, sought to create, circulate, preserve, and sometimes even destroy books.

Wells Cathedral Library obviously has its own rich history as a library but, thanks to the work of its librarian, Kevin Spears, we are now able to hear about many of the stories that lie behind the books on its shelves. In nineteen engaging and informative chapters, Spears introduces us to a wealth of topics, from the broadest questions regarding literacy and the transition from manuscript to print, to more focused subjects such as the printers' marks and the development of the book review. There are also chapters specifically about cathedral libraries, bibles, and the Book of Common Prayer. It is copiously illustrated, often drawing on the library's own collection.

This is a work of impressive synthesis from which I learned a lot, but it wears its own scholarship lightly. As someone who teaches the 'history of the book' to undergraduates, I found this an excellent general primer, but it will also serve as an invaluable introduction to any visitor to the library. The prophet may have lamented that 'of making books there is no end' but here is one book that I think deserves to be seen as a model for other libraries seeking to promote public understanding about their collections.

Professor Ian Gadd,
Bath Spa University

CHAPTER ONE

Why does the Cathedral have a Library?

ELIGIOUS FOUNDATIONS such as monasteries and cathedrals have always had a role in teaching and learning. The oldest schools in England have links to cathedrals: The King's School, Canterbury AD 597; King's School, Rochester, AD 604; and the Minster School, York, AD 627. Wells Cathedral School dates its foundation from AD 909 and has developed from the original school for choristers and the grammar school. In Europe, many of the early universities founded about AD 1150 grew from cathedral schools, eg: Paris and Salamanca.

Although a generalisation, monasteries were usually located in fairly remote rural areas. They lost their pre-eminence in education when the evolution of the feudal system and improvements in agriculture led to greater urbanisation, and it was the cathedrals, which were primarily built in the cities, which took over the growing educational needs for an administrative elite as well as the clergy. This was happening about AD 1100 throughout much of Europe which is also the time when new thinking and mathematical improvements enabled Gothic architecture to replace the Romanesque.

Cathedrals would have needed books from the earliest days for devotional and liturgical purposes as well as books of canon law to guide the administration. And because cathedrals were also seats of learning, they would have needed a slightly wider range of books to guide the tutors in interpreting the Bible and theological matters. Since at least the thirteenth century, the Chancellor of the cathedral has had the responsibility for giving lectures on theology and responsibility for the books in the cathedral.

Were cathedrals and monasteries not the same thing at one stage?

This is a slightly complicated area. All cathedrals were home to a religious community. However, some of the cathedrals were maintained by monks with a prior as their leader. The nine early monastic cathedrals were:

Canterbury	Durham	Rochester
Carlisle	Ely	Winchester
Coventry	Norwich	Worcester

All of these monastic cathedrals followed the rule of St. Benedict except Carlisle which was Augustinian. In addition, when Henry VIII dissolved the monasteries at the time of the Reformation, he agreed that a number of monasteries could avoid destruction if they evicted the monks and changed to being the home of a group of secular priests. These 'NEW FOUNDATION' cathedrals, as they were called, were founded between 1540 and 1542:

Bristol	Gloucester	Peterborough
Chester	Oxford	Westminster

All of these originally monastic cathedrals would have had libraries and also scriptoria where the monks would have copied books by hand. The other cathedrals were home to a community of canons and were called, somewhat confusingly, secular cathedrals:

Chichester	Lichfield	Salisbury
Exeter	Lincoln	Wells
Hereford	St Paul's	York

Secular cathedrals never had scriptoria for producing books and so all of the books for their libraries had to be acquired by purchase, or more normally, by gift.

A number of other cathedrals were created later:

Ripon (1836)	Wakefield (1888)	Chelmsford (1914)	Derby (1927)
Manchester (1847)	Liverpool (1904)	Coventry (re-established in 1918 after the See had moved to Lichfield in 1539)	Leicester (1927)
St Alban's (1877)	Southwark (1905)		Portsmouth (1927)
Truro (1880)	Birmingham (1905)	Bradford (1919)	Guildford (1965)
Newcastle (1882)	Sheffield (1914)	Blackburn (1926)	
Southwell (1884)	Bury St Edmunds (1914)		

If the library was not built until the 1450s, where were the books kept before that?

Before the invention of printing books with movable type in 1455, all books were written by hand, usually on animal skin known as parchment or vellum, but sometimes on paper. They were scarce and valuable. Because of their value, they were kept in locked wooden boxes that were heavy and rested on the floor, or they were kept in locked wooden cupboards that were often found in the cloisters of the monastic cathedrals. Large wooden chests for books have survived at Hereford cathedral. Lockable individual book boxes attached to the walls survive at Exeter cathedral.

Here at Wells we know from documents in the Archives that books were originally stored downstairs,

Medieval book chest

probably in the area now occupied by the Virgers' office. The first recording of this location is 1298 and we know that the Dean of Salisbury had already borrowed books by 1291. We have no remains of our original book furniture before 1450.

What made the cathedral decide to build the current library space?

In the case of Wells, Bishop Nicholas Bubwith gave the money to build the library over the entire almost 50 metre length (164 feet) of the East Cloister in his will of 1424. Although this was still before printed books, the demand from the rise of universities and professions had led to a greater supply of manuscript books. The need for more space in which to house the growing collections, together with the desire for a quiet space for study, had led a number of other cathedrals and Oxbridge colleges to find a suitable space for their books and call it a library.

The fifteenth century is the great time of library building in England. To gauge where we come in this development the following table gives approximate dates when other libraries were given a separate space of their own:

Cathedral Library approximate opening date	Year	Oxford or Cambridge College Library approximate opening date	Year
Hereford	1394	Merton College, Oxford	1379
Exeter	1413	New College, Oxford	1386
York	1422	Lincoln College, Oxford	1427
Lincoln	1426	Balliol College, Oxford	1431
Canterbury	1443	Durham College, Oxford	1431
Salisbury	1445	All Souls, Oxford	1438
Durham	1446	University College, Oxford	1440
St Albans	1452	Oriel College, Oxford	1444
Wells	1458	Queens College, Cambridge	1448
Worcester	1464	Pembroke College, Cambridge	1452
Lichfield	1489	Magdalen College, Oxford	1458

But surely libraries had existed before the fifteenth century?

Large libraries had existed from about 650 BC with Assurbanipal's royal library at Nineveh filled with clay tablets and cuneiform writing. In Classical times there were great libraries at Alexandria and Pergamum. In the Roman Empire libraries were numerous and often available to the public. But the demise of Roman rule in the West led to a long period of the Dark Ages when much of the knowledge of ancient Greece and Rome was effectively lost. It was partly preserved by eastern Christianity in Constantinople and also in the famous Islamic libraries of Baghdad, Cairo, Cordoba and Toledo. These Islamic libraries also stored the advances of Muslim scientists and mathematicians which were largely unknown in the West.

During all this time in western Europe, it was only the monastic, and to a lesser extent the secular cathedral libraries, that kept for future generations the few rare texts of Classical civilisation that had survived and enabled copies to be made in scriptoria. Until the growth of universities from about AD 1150, the only libraries in the West were these religious libraries which gave them an importance somewhat lost during later centuries.

Are all cathedral libraries the same?

As we have seen, they are amongst the oldest libraries in the country and many have very rich collections of manuscript and printed books.

However, there is wide variation in the collections. It would be expected that the monastic cathedrals would have lost their libraries at the Reformation, and some did. But others like Canterbury, Durham, Winchester and Worcester retained their most treasured manuscript and printed books and often their early music. Similarly, history would indicate that the libraries of the secular cathedrals would have survived intact, but Wells lost its library as Thomas Cromwell was the lay Dean of the cathedral and all books were surrendered to him as they were Catholic. St. Paul's lost its library in the Great Fire of London in 1666 and Lichfield lost its library in the damage done during several sieges in the Civil War of the 1640s. Bristol cathedral lost its library in the rioting in the city during 1831. Peterborough and Ely have physically transferred their libraries in large part to the safekeeping of Cambridge University.

The more modern collections in the libraries also differ widely. Hereford and Norwich cathedrals maintain lending collections of theological material for use in the diocese. At Wells this work is done by the Diocesan Resource Centre across the road, which has allowed us to focus our collection on interpreting the cathedral itself through books and journals on the fabric and history of the building and the people who have influenced it as well as books putting this work in historical context. Durham has a similar focus for its modern collection.

What makes them distinctive in terms of other libraries?

One major distinguishing factor is that cathedral libraries have all been heavily dependent on donations of books from the canons, at least from the Reformation. Most of them have received significant personal libraries numbering hundreds of books from their bishops at various times and a steady trickle of gifts from the canons. This means that most of the books in our libraries have a link to a specific benefactor and so we know when the book arrived and who gave it. And because the canons were the most educated people of their day and had wide interests, it gives us a range of books not only on theology, but also on science, medicine, poetry, languages, history, travel, etc.

Being dependent on donations has meant that there was never a clear stock selection policy, and so the sheer variety of books is one of the great charms of the collection. For example, Wells was the first library in the country to have a copy of Dante's *Divine Comedy* which arrived in 1418 as a gift from Bishop Bubwith. Bubwith had attended the Council of Constance in Germany from 1414-1418 and met there an Italian enthusiast for the works of Dante, Giovani Bertoldi de Serravalle who was Bishop of Firmano. Bertoldi was persuaded to translate Dante's work from Italian to Latin and this was done during the Council so that Bubwith brought a copy home with him. Unfortunately, although John Leland records seeing the copy on his visit in the 1530s, the book was one of those surrendered to Thomas Cromwell and it was lost.

Dante Alighieri

Two other examples to show how idiosyncratic but important the Chained Library collection is. Dean William Turner was the Dean of Wells either side of the Catholic Queen Mary who was on the throne from 1553-58. Turner, like most Protestant divines was forced to flee to Europe to escape imprisonment or execution. He fled with a Polish cleric called John à Lasco to whom Erasmus had sold his library on condition that Erasmus could use the books until he died. During their time together in Emden, Turner bought the five volume set of Aristotle's works printed in Greek by Aldus Manutius in Venice between 1495-8. Each volume is signed by Erasmus in Latin at the front and in Greek at the back with the signature saying he was Erasmus of Rotterdam

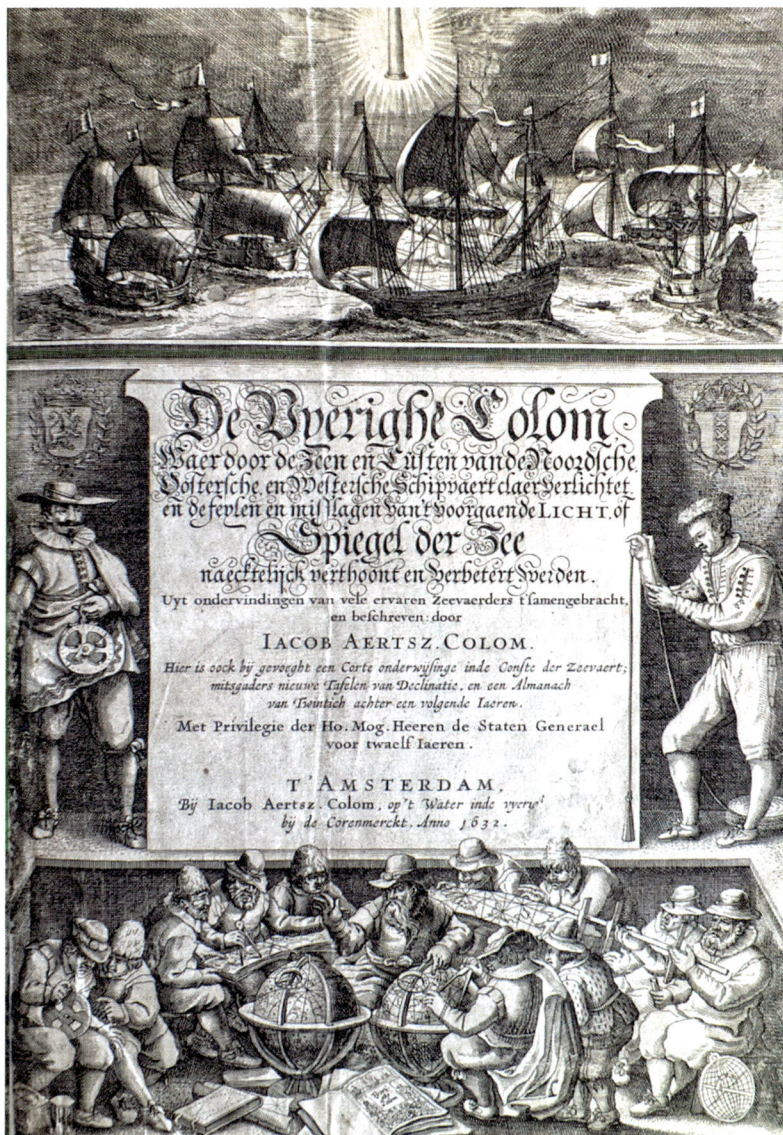

Title page of sea charts of the North Sea, printed by Jacob Colom in Amsterdam in 1632.

[*see photograph in Chapter Five*]. This set was given to the library in 1568 along with Turner's own *Herball* which was published in the same year. The *Herball* is regarded as one of the earliest books of botany written in English and Turner is spoken of as the Father of English Botany.

On the shelves opposite the set of Aristotle's work is a book of sea charts of the North Sea printed in Amsterdam in 1632. No librarian at Wells would ever have selected such a volume for acquisition. It is here

7

because Bishop Robert Creighton (1670-2) was actively building up the library when it returned from St. Cuthbert's church at the Restoration in May 1661. He asked all his friends and relatives to give books. His son-in-law, Francis Paulet of Hinton St. George in Somerset, had been a sea captain and so he contributed this book which still has the initials F P on the spine.

The only other libraries that have such rich and varied collections are in the Oxbridge colleges, the royal libraries, and the libraries of schools like Eton and Winchester.

Is any of this relevant in the 21st century?

The modern collection at Wells, books published after 1800, is actively used by the Guides and volunteers who help interpret the cathedral for visitors. Members of the Chapter can borrow books. The Chained Library collection of 4,000 books is largely a museum in that no-one comes to read the books, but biographers and students of the history of the book make good use of it. Because we know who owned the books, what is known as provenance, makes the collection especially valuable to biographers who will come to look at the notes the owner wrote in the book. A good example is the works of St. John of Damascus, printed in 1512, that belonged to Archbishop Thomas Cranmer, which has his beautiful handwriting throughout in red ink.

The biographer of Richard Busby, who was Headmaster of Westminster School and also the Treasurer

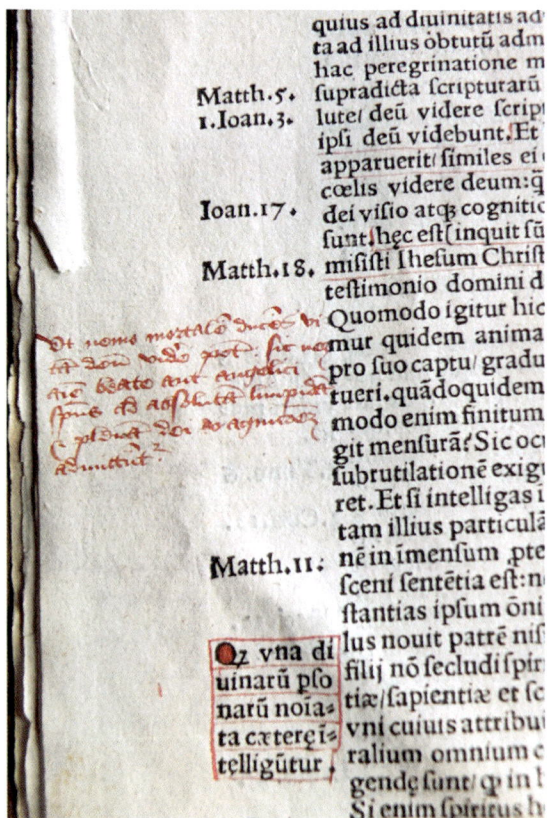

Thomas Cranmer's handwriting

of Wells cathedral who gave the money for the new library furniture installed in 1685, came recently to look at the books Busby gave to the cathedral and to the church in Martock.

The history of the book has become an established subject of study at universities and here it is the book as a physical object that interests the students. We have had scholars coming to look at the bindings of books and to examine the watermarks of paper in specific volumes. Students from Bath Spa university studying a module on the history of the book come each year to be guided by Professor Ian Gadd. We receive requests from academics worldwide to examine copies of particular books and send photographs, eg: the recent international survey of all remaining copies of the famous early book of anatomy by Vesalius published in the sixteenth century.

We also use the collection to assist schools studying the Reformation where we show our Hailes Psalter, a manuscript book written in 1514 which was smuggled out of the abbey at Hailes in Gloucestershire when the king's commissioners came to dissolve it on Christmas Eve 1539. Children learn that the book was written by hand, on animal skin, in Latin, and so was a Catholic book. They contrast this with the 1541 Great Bible which is printed on paper in English and reflect on the importance of printing to the success of the Protestant Reformation.

And the visitors to the cathedral who make it up to the library are intrigued to see chained books and to hear more about the library's history. They realise that a working library that is still in the same location in which it started some 560 years ago is something rare and special. Whilst the Chained Library may no longer be used as a resource for the Cathedral Chapter to aid their learning, it has an active future as a 'memory institution' for researchers and visitors alike.

WHERE CAN I READ MORE ABOUT THIS?

BATTLES, MATTHEW – *Library: an unquiet history* – Heinemann, 2003

BOTFIELD, BERIAH – *Notes on the Cathedral Libraries of England* –
   Pickering, 1849, (in the Reading Room at 027)

CAMBRIDGE HISTORY LIBRARIES IN BRITAIN AND IRELAND, Vols.I and II
   Cambridge University Press [CUP], 2006

CANNON, JON – *Cathedral: the great English cathedrals and the world that
   made them, 600-1450* – Constable, 2007, (in the Reading Room at 726.6)

IRWIN, RAYMOND – *The English Library* – Allen & Unwin, 1966

REYNOLDS, HERBERT – *Our Cathedral Libraries: conference paper* – 1879
   (in the Reading Room at 026)

SAVAGE, F.A. – *Old English Libraries* – Methuen, 1911

WALLACE, DAVID – *Dante in Somerset* – in New Medieval Literatures Vol.III,
   1999, pp.9-38

WORMALD, FRANCIS and WRIGHT, C.E. – *The English Library Before 1700*
   – University of London Press, 1958

CHAPTER TWO

Lecterns, Stalls and Chains

Why did the early library have lecterns and not shelves for the books?

WHEN THE LIBRARY first opened in about 1458, it would not have contained many books. With printing only developed by Gutenberg in 1455 in Germany, printed books were still not available. All books at the time the library opened were manuscript books written by hand on parchment and so scarce. Although we have no catalogue of the early library, when Henry VIII's antiquarian, John Leland, visited Wells cathedral in the 1530s, he noted forty-six books of particular significance*. And from that list, and comparing our library to others where stock totals of the time were known, you could estimate that the library would still have only had about 150 books in total some 100 years after it opened. So the practice of the day was to lay books out flat on a shelf or lectern. Effectively, book shelves had not been invented as the number of books did not require them.

Original library lectern

We do have some books that can be identified as having been bound for lectern use as they have metal studs or bosses on the front and back boards (made of wood) to protect the leather when placed flat. An example is this 1583 copy of Foxe's *Book of Martyrs*.

---

* If anyone wants to know which were the forty-six books, they are listed starting on page 116 in WILLIAMS, THOMAS – *Somerset Medieval Libraries* (in the Reading Room shelved at 027).

Books with such metal bosses do not fit well on book shelves as they take too much space and damage the binding of adjacent books.

Is the lectern in the Reading Room from the first library?

We assume so but there is no proof. Circumstantial evidence is that the design and metal fittings are the same as the furniture in the Vicars' Hall and Treasury which were built at much the same time that the library opened. But the Vicars also had a library above their chapel and it may have come from there. We can say that it is definitely from Wells cathedral and it was made in the fifteenth century.

Lectern book: Foxe's *Book of Martyrs*

We know that the lectern had its legs shortened in fairly recent memory. This is a shame as its design leaves some doubt as to whether it was designed for people to read standing up or sitting down. There are some contemporary French standing lecterns with cupboards and the University of Leiden had standing lecterns but of a later date. These were favoured where space was in short supply as you can fit more of them in as there is no seating. But space was not a problem in Wells as it probably had the largest Medieval library in the country. Seated lecterns would normally have space to put your legs underneath rather than blocking them with a cupboard. It is also highly likely that a metal rod fitted between the finials at the top and that books were chained to the rod. Seated lecterns often had a shelf underneath for the chained books not being read to be rested on and when we say that people could put such books in the cupboard we are almost certainly wrong as the chain would stop the door being closed.

So it is a venerable and treasured piece of furniture, and one of only a handful of Medieval lecterns left in the country, but we cannot say with any authority how it was used except that it would have fitted between the windows. The numerous and evenly spaced windows are the indication of a Medieval lectern library.

Are there any libraries in the world that still use lecterns for their books?

There are none in Britain although Lincoln cathedral library also has a couple of lecterns remaining from their early library. The best example of a lectern library is at St. Walburga's church at Zutphen in the Netherlands shown in the photo below. This dates from 1555 showing that lecterns were still favoured 100 years after Wells cathedral's library was opened.

St. Walburga's, Zutphen

Another rare example of a lectern library is the Biblioteca Malatestiana at Cesena in Italy which dates from 1452.

When did the library move to shelves rather than lecterns?

By the time of the English Civil War, printed books were readily available and the library had been functioning for 200 years. It had outgrown the capacity to lay books out on lecterns. We know very little about the library in the seventeenth century except that at the Restoration, the books that had been taken to St. Cuthbert's church when the cathedral was closed for fifteen years during the Commonwealth, were returned on 14th May 1661 and that there were some 200 books returned. Shortly after that, Richard Busby, who was the Treasurer of Wells cathedral but better known as the Headmaster of Westminster School, gave money for the "beautification" of the library. This donation allowed the Chapter to put down oak floor boards, some of them recycled oak from the now redundant lecterns, and to build the pinewood shelves and benches in 1685.

More details of the donations and refurbishing are in the booklet on the history of the library that we sell in the Reading Room and Shop.

How did they fit the much larger book shelves into the same space?

The main problem was the small space between the windows which was ideal for the lecterns. At Merton College, Oxford (a library even older than ours, having moved to its current space in 1379) they replaced the lecterns in the late sixteenth century with single-sided book shelves which still fitted between the windows. They then had the problem that the height of the shelves blocked out too much light. So they had to put in dormer windows which was done in 1590 and 1624.

Merton College library

Here at Wells we adopted a different solution: blocking up every alternate window to accommodate the new presses. These presses have shelves that are deeper than really necessary, but they are that way because of the space left when you have to fit them between alternate windows. You can clearly see the blocked in windows walking across the Palm Courtyard from the New Entry Cloister.

With books chained you have to put in a bench to rest the book on and a seat. Chains have to be of three different lengths with the longest for a book on the top shelf. The combination of shelves with a bench to rest the books on and a seat is known as the stall system and all chained libraries have the same configuration after chained lecterns were superseded.

West facing side of Wells cathedral library, showing blocked in windows.

Why are book-presses so called?

I have never found a completely satisfactory answer. The term 'press' seems to have entered the English language from the early French and means any form of cupboard with shelves for storage. We also used to have linen-presses for storing bed linen or table cloths. *The Oxford English Dictionary* has a first quotation of 1611 for the term book-press. Confusingly, modern day bookbinders also have book presses which are screw tightened devices to make an unbound book more compact. And then there is a printing press…

Why did some of the books need chaining if they were printed?

It is not clear why the then Dean, Dr. Ralph Bathurst, would have wished to make a chained library as late as 1685. The cathedral's library is a private library only open to the Chapter and the canons so theft was unlikely to have been a problem. Chains had been taken off books at most Cambridge colleges by 1650 as they impeded access, damaged the bindings of neighbouring books, and made it harder to move them round. And printed books were no longer so rare and valuable as manuscript books had been. But Bathurst was an Oxford man where the chains remained for longer, eg: the Duke Humfrey's library's chains were not removed until 1760.

The design of the book-presses is based on those at Corpus Christi College and the latticed wooden covers on the half shelves for smaller books is based on those at another Oxford College, Merton. Only 300 books were ever chained at Wells. Some would have been already chained from the lectern days. Others may well have been given to the library by canons on the condition that they be chained in perpetuity to remember the donor, rather like a chantry chapel. The chaining was continued until 1735 from records kept in the Archives. Chains were made from hot forged steel which was then dipped in a mix containing linseed oil to prevent them rusting. The chains have swivels built in to make it easier to keep them out of the way when opening books.

Chains with swivel

Doesn't it seem wrong to chain books up?

It would today but not 600 years ago when libraries in this country were still a novelty. Before that, books were kept in big wooden boxes resting on the floor [*see photo in Chapter One*] which often had three padlocks and three different people had the keys. The chained library was an innovative and liberating solution to this problem. Readers no longer had to assemble all three people with their keys to retrieve a book as they could enter the library and find what they wanted to read but the book was still secure as it was chained. Chaining ensured easier access to books.

Why are the books back to front?

Mainly because the best place to chain a book is on one of the front or back boards which are quite solid. The spine would be likely to tear or pull away from the binding if the chain was attached to it. Besides, spines did not have authors and titles written on them until about the 1570s, and not commonly until 100 years after that. Books laid out flat on lecterns did not have anything written on their spines because the spines were not seen, only the front cover which had bosses and other decoration. It took some time for spine decoration to become common.

How do you know which books are which then?

Another reason that books remained back to front was that their small numbers made them fairly easy to identify. If you think of a kitchen, very often containers of tea, sugar or flour are unlabelled because we recognise them by shape, size and colour. More plentiful items like spice jars have to be labelled to find what you need more quickly. So early readers would often know what they wanted just by recognising the book by its size and where they usually found it. The system most chained libraries had was to note the books on each shelf with a list attached to the end of the bay of shelves. Examples can be seen at Hereford cathedral's library or on its website. And some books had a brief author or title written on the fore-edge, eg: *Damascene* to tell us that G 3/19 is the work of St. John of Damascus.

Libraries in those days kept books arranged by press-marks which gives each book a coded number that did not change as the books were not moved once they were added. Here at Wells each bay was given a letter of the alphabet; then every bottom shelf was numbered 1, the middle shelf 2 and the top shelf 3.

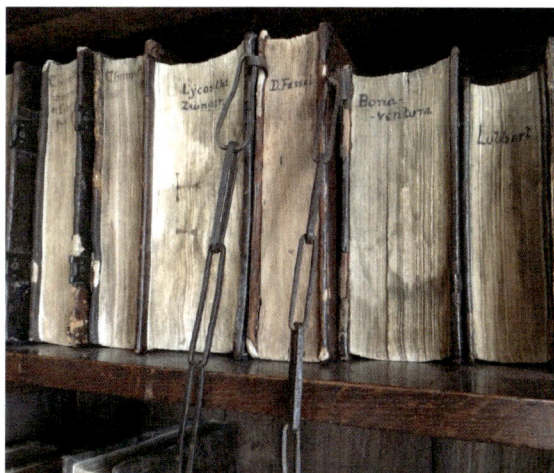

Fore-edge labels on books at the Francis Trigge library, St. Wulfram's church, Grantham.
(photo courtesy of Denise Sowden https://www.denisesowden.com/#)

As a book was added it was simply given a running number from the aisle to the window. So a book listed as G 3/19 is found by going to bay G, looking on the top shelf and locating the nineteenth book along. Our earliest catalogue is a hand-written one in two books that dates from 1734. And in most cases, the press-marks recorded in the catalogue of 1734 are where you will still find the book today. Amazon uses a similar system in its warehouses and it works. The catch is that books on the same subject will not necessarily be found together. That gave people like Melvil Dewey the opportunity to design subject classification schemes for books in the nineteenth century.

When did books start to have authors and titles noted on their spines?

As printed books became more plentiful, individuals were acquiring quite large libraries. Many of them liked to bind their books in the same colour and design of leather so that they all looked alike. This led to the custom of lettering details on the spine. This began in the late sixteenth century. [*See also Chapter Eighteen on Bookbinding*]

Are there any other chained libraries in England?

There are only a handful. Hereford cathedral is the best known and all its books are chained. It is no longer in its original location but in a modern building with full climate control. Wimborne Minster in Dorset has a small library in its old Treasury but again all the books are chained. Neither of these have the original chains on the books. There is also the Francis Trigge library in St. Wulfram's church in Grantham and a few ancient grammar schools have small collections, often in cupboards in the headmaster's study. Chetham's library in Manchester has an example of a cupboard of chained books from a local parish library. Some Oxbridge libraries keep a few books chained as a historical curiosity, eg: Merton.

WHERE CAN I READ MORE ABOUT THIS?

Here in the Reading Room we have the excellent and recent *The Library: a world history* by DR. JAMES CAMPBELL who is a Cambridge architectural historian. Chapter 3 of this beautifully illustrated book features Wells cathedral library and Merton College Oxford as two libraries in continuous use for over 500 years that have had to adapt their architecture to accommodate the change from lecterns to stalls. This book is usually on display on the shelves to the left.

ALSO IN THE READING ROOM YOU WILL FIND:

BLADES, WILLIAM – *Books in Chains* Elliot Stock, 1892 (in the Reading Room at 026)

CLARK, JOHN – *Care of Books* – Cambridge University Press, 1909 (in the Reading Room at 020)

PETROSKI, HENRY – *The Book on the Bookshelf* – Knopf, 1999, (in the Reading Room at 022)

STREETER, BURNETT – *The Chained Library* – Macmillan, 1931, (in the Reading Room at 026)

WILLIAMS, THOMAS – *Somerset Medieval Libraries* – Arrowsmith, 1897, (in the Reading Room at 027)

CHAPTER THREE

Producing Manuscript Books

Was it only monks who produced manuscript books?

ALL BOOKS WERE HANDWRITTEN before 1455 when printing with moveable type was introduced. Until about 1100, most of these were produced in religious houses. But as universities came into being in Paris, Bologna, and Oxford in the 1100s, demand for books increased. Professional scribes would undertake to make copies of books and often the university would hire out approved pages of a set book to be copied. As well as academics, doctors and lawyers also required books. Within a short time there was a commercial trade in manuscript books and monks would often contract out their book production rather than write the books within the monastery. By 1300, most books were commercially produced.

Are parchment and vellum the same thing?

Technically, vellum is the skin of a calf whereas parchment refers to the prepared skin of any animal. In western Europe sheepskin was common but in Italy it might be goatskin that was made into parchment. It often takes an expert to say which animal was the origin of a piece of parchment and the two terms are interchangeable without any real harm to scholarship.

How many animal skins would be used in a book?

Animals were killed for food and not just for making parchment. How many skins were used in a book depends on its size and length, but the British Library estimates that 170 calf skins were used for making each one of the forty-five copies of Gutenberg's Bible printed on vellum. Printing was mostly on paper but deluxe editions are known in parchment and even everyday schoolbooks were thought to be more hardwearing if printed on rough quality parchment. And by the 1400s many manuscript books were written on paper so there is not a clear division between the use of the two materials.

How was the skin of an animal prepared before being written on?

The skin would be soaked in a solution of lime and water in a vat for about a week to loosen the hair. It would then be scraped to remove the hair and the outer layer of skin before another soaking for two days in clean water to rinse out the lime. The skin is then stretched out taut on a wooden frame to dry. The finer scraping of the skin then begins with a rounded knife called a lunellum and continues until the parchmenter has the required fineness.

Preparing the skin

In 1492 Johannes Trithemius, the Abbot of Sponheim, wrote a polemic against printing saying that paper would only last for a couple of hundred years whereas parchment would last a thousand. It is true that good parchment will last for a thousand years, we have a document in the cathedral archives dating from AD 958, but the paper in our incunabula is now over 500 years old and lasting well.

Scraping the skin

What was the ink made from?

There were two types of ink used on parchment after it had been rubbed with chalk to prepare it for writing on. Carbon ink is made from charcoal or lamp-black mixed with gum and was in use in earlier periods. It has the disadvantage of being fairly easy to rub off.

Metal-gall ink was preferred in later periods. The principal ingredient is the oak apple, the ball-like growth on the twigs and leaves of oak trees resulting from a gall wasp laying its eggs in the growing

Oak apples

bud of the tree. The larva grows into an insect which bores its way out leaving a hard oak apple the size of a marble.

The oak apples are crushed and soaked in vinegar or white wine. They are then added to ferrous sulphate or copperas which occurs naturally in some soils, or by adding sulphuric acid to old nails. Some gum arabic, the dried-up sap of the acacia tree, is then added and the mixture will go from a pale brown to black. It will darken further on exposure to air and soaks well into parchment as well as being translucent and shinier than carbon ink.

Red ink was made from vermilion, which is mercuric sulphide, added to egg white and gum arabic. It could also be made from chips of brazilwood soaked in vinegar or urine.

How were quill pens made?

Quill pens were made from the five outer wing feathers of a goose.

Recently plucked feathers are too flexible and have to be left to harden or soaked in water and then plunged in a tray of heated sand. A penknife is used to pare back the tube to a nib which is then slit up the centre. A scribe would constant-ly have to re-sharpen the nib as the slit will open with

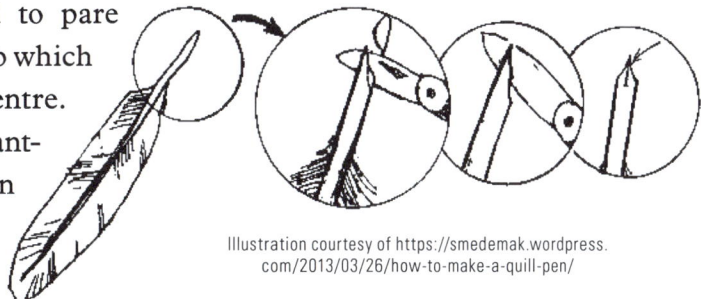

Illustration courtesy of https://smedemak.wordpress.com/2013/03/26/how-to-make-a-quill-pen/

use, and anything up to sixty times in a working day was to be expected. The pens were dipped in an inkhorn.

What was used for the coloured decoration of many manuscript books?

One of the delights of manuscript books is that each one is unique and the level of ornamentation will vary. The least decorated will usually have ornamental and enlarged initial capital letters on the first page and these may have borders with ivy and acanthus leaves interspersed with rabbits, birds, etc. These can be in colour and illuminated with gold. More elaborate books will have miniature paintings as well.

Such decoration was always added after the scribe had written the text. It was normal for the task of decorating and illuminating to be done by an artist other than the scribe and even this task would be sub-divided so that one person might draw the design, another paint on the colour and another do the gold illumination. All this presupposes that a page layout had been decided according to how much the client was willing to pay and often pattern books were used to help choose the design.

Illuminated capital letter in the Hailes psalter.

If gold is to be used, and technically manuscripts are only referred to as illuminated if gold or silver are used, it would be applied before any colour is painted on. This is because gold will adhere to any pigment and so ruin the design. Also, if the gold is to be burnished, usually by rubbing it vigorously with a dog's tooth, it will smudge any painting already around it. Gold leaf was the most common way of adding gold.

A wet glue would be applied to the parchment and the gold leaf laid on top. Later in the fifteenth century, powdered gold was made into a form of ink by mixing it with gum arabic, but this was more expensive as it used more gold. However, the powdered gold ink could be applied after the colour and gave a frosted finish.

The coloured paint was made from either minerals or vegetable dyes and usually applied with a brush but sometimes a pen. Red could be made from cinnabar or mercuric sulphide found in Spain and other Mediterranean countries or from plants such as madder or the shrub *Pherocarpus draco*. Blue was often crushed azurite, also found in Spain, but could be from the crushed seeds of *Crozophora*. The most prized blue was from lapis lazuli coming from Afghanistan. Green was made from malachite or verdigris, the green patina that forms on copper. Yellow came from volcanic earth and white from white lead.

Why are scribes usually shown with both a pen and another instrument in the other hand?

The other instrument is a pointed knife which is used both to scrape away any mistakes, but also to hold the parchment flat for the pen being used by the other hand.

How were the lines drawn on the parchment to keep the text straight?

Until the twelfth century, manuscripts tended to have the lines ruled in drypoint, ie scored with the back of a knife or a stylus. Later, it was the fashion to have the lines visibly ruled and some

Eadwine the scribe

early printed books did the same. To save doing this for each page, it was common to rule out the top page and then make pin holes at the end of each line so that they transferred to several pieces of parchment below. These are known as prickmarks and we have several of our manuscript books with clear prickmarks; the fragment of the Benedictine Rule dating from about AD 1100 shows them clearly.

Professional scribes might have a spiked metal wheel to make the marks. When books were bound these were often trimmed off so we are fortunate to have examples.

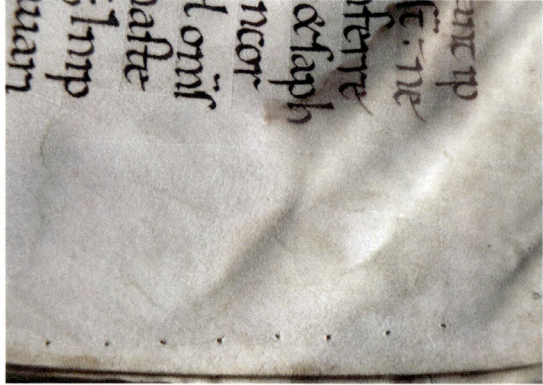

Prickmarks

How long did it take someone to write a book by hand?

Monks would be slower simply because they had to fit the rounds of prayer and other monastic duties into their daily timetable. Perhaps three or four books a year would be an average for a monk depending on the size of the book and the time of year. The lack of daylight in winter would reduce their productivity.

Professional scribes paid by the job would be considerably faster. A Book of Hours could be written in a week, and the decoration done after that, but perhaps a month for each book is a better average. Scribes were not always happy with their lot and sometimes appended comments to their script. Collected examples include:

- *Writing is excessive drudgery. It crooks your back, it dims your sight, it twists your stomach, and your sides.*
- *St. Patrick of Armagh, deliver me from writing.*
- *As the sick man desireth health even so doth the scribe desire the end of the volume.*
- *Now I've written the whole thing: for Christ's sake give me a drink.*

WHERE CAN I READ MORE ABOUT THIS?

AVRIN, LEILA – *Scribes, Scripts and Books* – British Library, 1991

DE HAMEL, CHRISTOPHER – *Scribes and Illuminators* – British Museum, 1992 (in the Reading Room at 709)

DE HAMEL, CHRISTOPHER – *A History of Illuminated Manuscripts* Phaidon, 1986, (in the Reading Room at 745.67)

CHAPTER FOUR

The Introduction of Paper

Is the paper in the Chained Library books handmade?

Y ES. All paper was handmade until the early 1800s and all books in the Chained Library were published before 1800. Papermaking requires a cellulose material: in the old days it was mainly rags from clothing, old sailcloth made of flax, or hemp from old rope. These raw materials had to be cleaned, softened and beaten before diluting in water to form a weak suspension. The suspended solution is then scooped out with a wire frame like a sieve which allows the water to run out but leaves a thin layer of fibres on the surface. This layer of matted fibres becomes the sheet of paper which is then drained, pressed and dried. It may then, or in the earlier process, be treated with additives to give it the right amount of hardness and gloss for the purpose it is intended for, ie banknotes, artists' printmaking, writing paper, etc. Without the 'sizing' of the surface it would be blotting paper.

Paper-making

Paper mills have always been located next to rivers giving a clean source of running water as large amounts of water are needed in the cleaning, beating and suspension stages. Better quality paper was made near cities as the supply of rags was more plentiful. Mills nearer the sea would tend to use sailcloth and ropes which made for poorer quality paper.

Are all printed books made of paper?

In the early days of printing, before and just after 1500, a few books were printed on parchment, ie animal skin, but very few. For example, the *Gutenberg Bible* printed in the 1450s is thought to have had 145 copies made on paper and forty-five on vellum. Vellum (parchment made from calves) is less absorbent than paper so the ink is likely to smudge in the printing process. It also takes longer to dry the ink. And vellum costs more than paper. But it was reckoned to be a harder wearing material and some school books were printed on low quality parchment, and a few 'luxury' editions were printed on good quality vellum. But, overwhelmingly, printing is associated with paper. As well as lower cost, paper had the advantages of uniformity of size and texture, superiority in remaining flat, and ease of cutting.

It should be noted that not all manuscript books are written on parchment. By the late fourteenth century some scribes were using paper. We have a manuscript book which is a commentary on the Clementine Constitutions written on paper made in Italy dated to the 1380s.

Did the paper come from the paper mills near Wells?

No. Paper has been made at Wookey since the early 1600s and is still made at St. Cuthbert's mill here in Wells, but this has tended to be writing paper or specialist papers for artists, lawyers, etc.

So where did the paper for books come from?

It was imported from France, Italy and the Netherlands. On the Continent, people wore more linen so the rags were ideal for paper making. Cotton is also good for making paper but cotton clothing really had to wait until the Industrial Revolution and the factories of the eighteenth and nineteenth centuries.

In the 1500s the imported paper was mainly French or Italian but in the 1600s it came more from Holland. The choice of provider was to some extent dependent upon who Britain was at war with at the time, and also the price paid. Paper was in those days at least 35-50% of the cost of production of a book.

Sorting rags

Why couldn't Britain make its own paper for books?

Paper making in Britain in the handmade days always had the problem of a scarcity of rags. It took 1.5kg of rags to make 1kg of paper. We tend to wear woollen clothes and you cannot make paper from wool. Paper mills were relatively plentiful (116 by 1700 in England) but they were mainly producing brown paper for packaging owing to the poor quality of the fibres from which the paper was made and the lack of a suitable bleach. Bleaching was time consuming requiring soaking in quick lime and using the sun's rays, which put England at a further disadvantage.

The earliest attempt to set up a paper mill for printing paper was as early as the 1490s and this was John Tate's Sele Mill near Hertford. It only survived until 1510 as the Continental paper producers slashed their prices to undercut him and force him out of business. (Similar practice can be observed even in 2015/6 as Saudi Arabia and OPEC slash the price of oil to make production from American shale uneconomic). European countries also banned exports of rags to protect their own industry.

The government was aware of the importance of assisting indigenous paper production and when John Spilman set up his paper mill in 1588 in Dartford, Kent, he had a 'privilege' from the Crown giving him a monopoly of rag purchasing. When James I visited his mill in 1605, Spilman was knighted. But even with these advantages, this mill went out of business in 1641.

When did things improve?

By 1720 England was about two-thirds self sufficient in paper production thanks partly to new paper mills in Scotland set up with German and French expertise. Also, the Hollander engine invented at the end of the seventeenth century replaced beating rags with blades to cut them. This was still water driven but increased productivity twelve times. By 1800 England was self sufficient in paper production.

When was wood pulp paper introduced?

In the early 1800s a number of developments took place:

1   Experiments were made using HAY, STRAW AND THISTLES to replace rags but these were not successful, in part as the paper was too yellow.

2   In 1839, ESPARTO GRASS was imported from Spain and North Africa to make the fibrous pulp and was moderately successful. It was not inexpensive but could produce good quality paper. (Winston Churchill favoured it for the printing of some of his books after World War II).

3   The Industrial Revolution brought STEAM POWER to replace water power and thus accelerated the production in various ways from beating to pressing.

4   CHLORINE BLEACH began production in 1800 which enabled whiter paper from pulp although at first it made very brittle paper that did not last.

5   By 1850 WOOD PULP had become the primary source for paper thanks to better bleach and steam power plus the readier availability of trees. It had been known since 1719 that paper could be made from wood pulp but there was no commercial process invented to make it practical at that time. The first book made of paper from wood pulp is thought to date from 1802.

6   Also, paper could be successfully RECYCLED from about 1800 when they discovered how to remove the ink and other impurities.

Modern paper making
Courtesy Hainan Jinhai Paper and Pulp Company http://www.appjh.com.cn/en/corp.html

How bad is the problem of foxing in the old books?

The reddish brown staining on paper called foxing hardly appears on paper in the books in the Chained Library. They were made of old-fashioned handmade paper which rarely shows signs of foxing unless the conditions of storage are inappropriate, eg: too damp. Foxing is associated more with the machine made paper developed from the 1800s. That said, a few early books produced on poor quality paper can show staining, eg: our 1568 copy of Dean William Turner's *Herball*.

How interesting is paper to book historians?

The sources of paper can be traced by their watermarks. A watermark is a design fashioned in wire which was sewn with even finer wire to the frame or sieve used in the papermaking process. Each mill would have its own design and this watermark can be seen as clearer when the paper is held up to a light source. Watermarks were introduced on paper made in Bologna, Italy, in 1282. Modern banknotes still use them.

Book historians can trace the source of the paper used by these watermarks and also use them to date the printing of a book. Paper tended to be used within 3-4 years of manufacture and as there were tiny differences in the wire designs used to replace ones that wore out, paper can be dated quite accurately. This can be helpful as printers did not always print a date on the book, especially in the earliest books before 1500.

A few years ago Professor Nicholas Pickwoad, probably Britain's foremost expert on bookbinding, came to our library to look at the watermarks in the eight volumes of the works of St. John Chrysostom published in Greek at Eton College in 1612 by Sir Henry Savile. In the binders' waste used to reinforce the binding of one volume he discovered the red stamps from the French paper mill that had supplied some of the paper. He said this was very rare and it does indicate the importance of our collection to book historians.

WHERE CAN I READ MORE ABOUT THIS?

There is no book in the Reading Room specifically on the subject but in the bound volumes of the Somerset Archaeological and Natural History Society's Proceedings of 2009 there is an article by BRIAN LUKER *Paper and papermakers around Wells* on pages 115-122.

Also:

HILLS, RICHARD – *Papermaking in Britain 1488-1988: a short history* – Athlone Press, 1988

MONRO, ALEXANDER – *The Paper Trail: an unexpected history of the world's greatest invention* – Allen Lane, 2014

CHAPTER FIVE

Development of Print

When did the printing of books begin?

THE PRINTING OF BOOKS with moveable type began with Gutenberg's Latin Bible, printed in Mainz in Germany in 1455. There is some debate as to whether or not books crudely printed from carved wooden blocks, so-called block books, using much the same techniques as printing patterns on textiles with wooden blocks, preceded printed books. The evidence tends to indicate that these were introduced at about the same time as printing. In any case, the wood on block books wore out quickly, the definition of letters was poor, and each page had to be carved separately, so that the future of books printed with moveable type was assured.

What was new about Gutenberg's printing?

The essential mechanism of a printing press was an adaptation of the wooden olive and wine presses that had existed for centuries. What was new was that the print was cast in metal and could be re-used over and over again, ie: moveable type. Johann Gutenberg (1398-1468) was a goldsmith, and so familiar with metal. Also, the ink previously used for

Printing shop of the seventeenth century

manuscripts or with block books would not adhere to metal and so a new ink had to be formulated. And paper rather than animal skin was the material normally used to print on.

How was the metal type made?

The most skilful task was that of the punch cutter who had to carve each letter to the exact size and chosen font design on a small bar of steel. This was then punched into softer copper to form a matrix of the correct design. A molten alloy of lead, tin and antimony was poured into the mould holding the matrix and when set, the stem of metal with a letter on the end was removed and would be ready to print with. It was calculated that an individual piece of type could be made every twelve seconds by experienced craftsmen. The earliest

Typefounder pouring lead alloy into a mould.

printers made their own type and usually had a background in metal working, but making type soon became a specialist trade so that printers bought in their requirements.

What was special about the ink?

Early printers had to experiment to find a formula that would stick to metal and yet transfer to the paper, not smudge easily, would fix on the paper and not rub off, and it had to dry as quickly as possible. Some twenty years earlier the artist Jan van Eyck had begun using oil paint; printing ink is an adapted version of artist's oil paint using soot, rosin and linseed oil.

How does all this become a printed page?

A printer would need a large number of metal sorts, ie: individual letters, numbers and punctuation marks, collectively called a fount of type before starting work. Common letters such as 'e' would be more numerous than the letter 'z', and the appropriate numbers were kept in wooden cabinets subdivided into pigeon holes each containing a separate individual character. The capital letters were separated into one case which was generally positioned above the box with normal letters and hence we have 'upper case' for capitals and 'lower case' for normal sized font. Later, a groove would be cut in the metal so that compositors could feel which was the correct way up to arrange the letters in a grooved metal stick, but early printers did not have this refinement and had to check by eye. Each stick would be loaded with words to form a line, then these would be loaded in a galley to form a page, and then the complete page was locked in a forme ready to be inked.

Early compositor

Ink was spread on the type using what looked like leather boxing gloves on a stick. A quantity of ink was poured on to a slab of stone and then the leather 'ball' stuffed with horsehair dabbed in it before pressing it on the metal type.

Once the type was inked, a piece of paper was placed on top and then the press brought down to evenly imprint the pattern of the page on the paper. Multiple copies would then be made up to the number required for the edition. The paper was then hung up to dry before any folding or cutting was done to

Preparing the forme and inking the type.

prepare the book for binding. The metal type could then be washed to remove the ink and the individual letters put back in their type-cases to be used again.

It is important for us to remember that every book in the Chained Library is hand-made. From the making of the wooden press, the cutting of the punch, to arranging the type, to making the ink and the paper, to then binding the book, every single activity is done by hand.

How quickly could a book be printed?

Obviously the size of the page and the length of the book are major variables, but an efficient printing workshop could print 180 pages in an hour which amounted to 2,500 single-sided sheets in a day or 1,500 double-sided.

What made printing a successful invention?

The relative speed of printing compared with the writing of books by hand, coupled with the lower cost of printing on paper, meant that books became more affordable and immediately available rather than comm-issioning a scribe to copy one. Printed books also had more consistency and errors could be corrected more neatly than scribes could achieve when they made errors in copying. By 1500, there were 282 towns and cities in Europe with printing presses. These had produced some 28,000 editions of books, pamphlets and broadsides amounting to approximately ten million copies. Of these, 77% were in Latin, 7% in Italian, 6% in German, 5% in French; and as to subjects: 45% were religious; 30% classical, medieval and contemporary literature; 10% legal and 10% scientific. All the scribes in Europe would have taken over a thousand years to produce the same number of books printed in these first forty-five years of printing.

Despite the advantages of lower cost, printed books were regarded as vulgar by many who were used to having manuscript books made specifically to their taste in terms of script and illustration. To overcome this resistance, many early printed books would leave the initial capitals blank so that customers could have them hand illustrated to make them look more like the manuscript books that they had been familiar with. An excellent example is our copy of Pliny the Elder's *Natural History*, printed by Nicholas Jenson in Venice in 1472:

Pliny: *Historiae Naturalis*, 1472

Many early printers would call on the same artists who still produced manuscript books to do this work.

Why are early printed books called incunabula?

An incunable (plural incunabula) is a book, broadside or pamphlet printed before the end of the year 1500. The word comes from the Latin meaning for cradle or swaddling clothes and denotes the early phase of printing. The term was first used in 1639 to describe early printed books.

What problems did early printers face?

- Compared with scribes who only needed a quill pen, ink and either paper or parchment, the printer had to make a large INVESTMENT in buying at least one fount of type, as well as the press, the more specialised ink, and a good quantity of paper which was often half of the cost of the finished book. With only one fount, a printer could not add chapter headings, marginalia, etc so they mainly had to buy several whereas a scribe could create endless variety with no extra investment.

- Whereas the scribe was commissioned to write a text with normally a guaranteed customer who paid on delivery of the finished article, the printer had to estimate how many copies of a book he would sell and then wait until a good proportion of them were sold before recovering the initial investment. Printers had to be cautious when estimating sales of a print run and editions of 200 or less were common in the early days. By 1489-90 editions were more commonly 400-500, and soon after 1,000 copies was not unusual. Many early printers failed after making the wrong calculations. Alternatively, making the right decisions could make them far more PROFIT than a scribe engaged in producing single copies.

- Type WORE OUT fairly quickly (after only four months in some cases) and had to be replaced. There was also no standardisation of size (the point system of measurement had to wait until the eighteenth century), or of the height of each metal sort. Part of the fascination of early books for scholars is seeing the variations between copies of an edition as different type was inserted to replace worn pieces.

- POOR QUALITY ink and the VARIABLE QUALITY AND SUPPLY of paper. Scholars have come to Wells to examine the different watermarks of the paper used in a single book to learn where it came from.

- These were dangerous times and whereas educational and legal text-books were safe to produce, political and religious books brought serious RISK OF OFFENCE and punishment by the authorities whether civil or religious.

- TRANSPORT of printed books also carried risk as the only options were either by road or water, usually in barrels, to protect the texts from water damage. To save weight, most books were sent unbound.

- Letting potential customers know what you had printed was difficult as there were no newspapers or book reviews. Sample pages could be posted outside your printing shop and rudimentary lists were circulated further afield. The annual Frankfurt Book Fair was set up very soon after printing began to bring together printers and booksellers, who were often the same person, and this event enabled them to PUBLICISE their current publications, see what the competition was doing, and take soundings on possible future books they could print.

- RECEIVING PAYMENT when books were exported was often lengthy and difficult. Books printed in Latin could be sold throughout Europe. An elaborate system of letters of credit was arranged as carrying cash was extremely hazardous, and the book fair had a major role in facilitating this form of settlement. However, the infrequency of fairs made payment slow.

How many incunabula do we have in the cathedral library at Wells?

We have eight incunabula in the Cathedral's collection and three in the Bath Abbey collection, and two very incomplete fragments of incunabula. That we lost our library at the time of the Reformation is shown by our neighbouring cathedrals which all have far more: Hereford sixty-three; Exeter forty-six; Worcester forty-two; Gloucester forty-two, and Salisbury forty-one. Our collection is listed on page ten of the pamphlet on the history of the library on sale in the library and

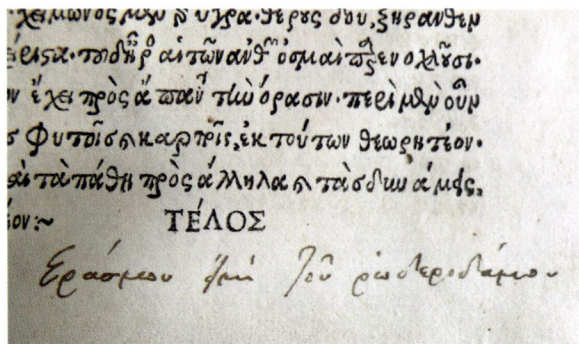

Signature of Erasmus in Greek

the shop. However, we do make up in quality what we lack in quantity with the set of five volumes of Aristotle's work in Greek, printed in Venice between 1495-8 by Aldus Manutius, that belonged to Erasmus and is signed by him in both Latin and Greek [*opposite page, bottom right*].

Pliny's *Historiae Naturalis* printed in Venice by Nicholas Jenson in 1472 is probably the most beautiful book in our collection.

WHERE CAN I READ MORE ABOUT THIS?

CHAPPELL, WARREN – *A Short History of the Printed Word* – Knopf, 1970

FEBVRE, LUCIEN and MARTIN, J. – *The Coming of the Book* – Verso, 1976

GASKELL, PHILIP – *A New Introduction to Bibliography* – Oxford University Press, 1972 (in the Reading Room at 010)

MAN, JOHN – *The Gutenberg Revolution* – Review, 2002

POTTEN,ED – *Emprynted in Thys Manere* – Cambridge University Press, 2014

Printing and the Mind of Man (exhibition catalogue) – 1963

STEINBERG, S.H. – *Five Hundred Years of Printing* – British Library, 1996

THORPE, JAMES – *The Gutenberg Bible* – Huntingdon Library, 1999

CHAPTER SIX

The Beginning of Printing in England

When did Caxton invent printing?

WILLIAM CAXTON (1422-91/2) did not invent printing, as we saw in the previous chapter, but he did introduce printing to England in 1476. Caxton had been living on the Continent for some years and had been effectively the leader of the British business community in Bruges. His business interests brought him into contact with Margaret, Duchess of Burgundy, the sister of Edward IV and Richard III, and in 1471 he retired from business to serve in her household. This brought travel to Cologne where he encountered printing. He acquired a printing press and translated the *Recuyll of the Historyes of Troye* which was then printed in Bruges in 1473, the first book ever printed in English.

Caxton showing Edward IV and his Queen specimens of his work.

In the autumn of 1476 he returned to England and set up a printing press next to Westminster Abbey so that he was near the court and Parliament and his royal and aristocratic patrons. Caxton was a literary figure and not just a printer. He saw that printing in Europe was well established and his main opportunity was to print books in English. In his fifteen years of printing he translated twenty-two works into English and printed some 108 books, mainly in English but a small proportion in Latin.

Caxton's contribution goes beyond printing in that he helped to standardise spelling which had varied greatly according to dialect. He promoted a late Middle English spelling which in his own day was becoming unfashionable and to him we owe the survival of anomalous spelling like the 'k' and 'gh' in knight. He also promoted English authors such as Geoffrey Chaucer's *Canterbury Tales* (1476/7), and Thomas Malory's *Morte Darthur* (1485).

Were printed books available in England before Caxton?

England was late in introducing printing and was something of a backwater with only the specialism of books in English to distinguish it. By Continental standards, English printing quality was poor. We have in the cathedral library the beautiful copy of Nicholas Jenson's Pliny the Elder's *Natural History* which was printed in Venice in 1472 and belonged to John Gunthorpe, who was the Dean of Wells from 1472-98.

The imported book trade really took off in the 1470s, with most books being in Latin from presses in Italy, Germany and France, but scholars and clerics had been able to import printed books from their networks on the Continent from the beginning of printing.

Was London the centre for printing?

When Caxton died in 1491/2, his printing workshop was taken over by his assistant Wynkyn de Worde after a three year legal battle. De Worde was probably a native of Alsace or he may have been Dutch. He had spotted that printing could be profitable if you printed more popular books in larger numbers. He moved the printing shop in 1500 from the elevated surroundings of Westminster to the City of London as he did not have Caxton's literary talents or network of patrons. De Worde chose to produce smaller books in larger quantities and his focus was on school primers for the grammar schools, and religious books such as breviaries, missals and psalters. He printed some 828 books before his death in 1534 and was the first printer to popularise the printing press in England. Julian Notary worked closely with de Worde specialising in printing in red and black.

In about 1478 Theodoric Rood started printing scholastic texts in Oxford. He printed a total of seventeen books. Another press was established at St. Albans but the name of the printer is not known.

The other presses were all in London. Best known is that of Richard Pynson (1488-1529) who specialised in religious and legal texts and after 1506 was styled Printer to the King as he printed statutes. John Lettou and Walter de Machlinia set up a press to print legal, religious and scholastic texts. It is noteworthy that apart from Caxton, all of these printers were born abroad: Julian Notary in Normandy, Pynson in France, Rood in Germany, Lettou probably in Lithuania, and Walter de Machlinia in Brabant.

To show how slow England was in developing printing, by 1500 there were five printers working in London whereas Venice had more than 100. Only 3% of books printed before 1500 were printed in England. In 1534 an Act was passed limiting the number of alien journeymen and apprentices to the book trade to encourage more Englishmen to take up the skills. However, this was as much an attempt to limit the import of heretical books as most of the foreign born printers were also importers.

Do we have any of their books in the Wells cathedral library?

The earliest ENGLISH printed book in the library belongs to Bath Abbey and is Wynkyn de Worde's 1493 edition of Voragine's *Golden Legend*. This book uses one of Caxton's types and is essentially a reprint of Caxton's earlier printing.

St. Andrew from *The Golden Legend*, printed by Wynkyn de Worde, 1493.

We also have Cuthbert Tunstall's *De Arte Supputandi* printed by Richard Pynson in 1522 [*right*]. Tunstall (1474-1559) was the Bishop of London who publicly burned copies of Tyndale's English translation of the Bible smuggled in from the Continent. This was the first book of mathematics printed in England and Tunstall based it on a similar book by Luca Pacioli that he had come across whilst a Humanist scholar in Italy. The frontispiece was engraved by Hans Holbein (1497-1543), hence the H H at the middle left. (Interestingly, to show how these woodcuts were often recycled, it also appears as the frame for a title page of a Bible printed in London in 1542 by Richard Bankes, which is in the Bath Abbey collection). The book by Tunstall belonged to Bishop George Hooper who was Bishop of Bath and Wells from 1704-1727.

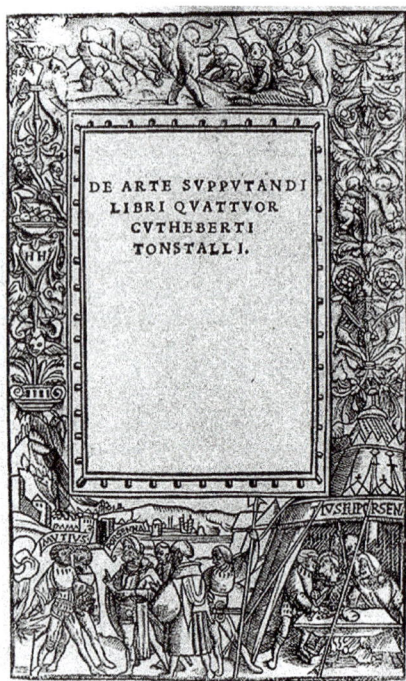

WHERE CAN I READ MORE ABOUT THIS?

BOFFEY, JULIA – *Manuscript and Print in London c.1475-1530* – British Library, 2012

CAMBRIDGE HISTORY OF THE BOOK IN BRITAIN, Vol.iii, 1400-1557 – Cambridge University Press [CUP], 2009

GILLESPIE, ALEXANDRA and WAKELIN, D. – *The Production of Books in England, 1350-1500* – CUP, 2011

GILLESPIE, VINCENT and POWELL, S. – *A Companion to the Early Printed Book in Britain 1476-1558* – Brewer, 2014

HELLINGA, LOTTE – *William Caxton and Early Printing in England* – British Library, 2010

HOTCHKISS, VALERIE and ROBINSON, F.– *English in Print: from Caxton to Shakespeare to Milton* – Illinois University Press, 2008

CHAPTER SEVEN

The Title Page

Surely a title page is just a bald statement of facts?

WE HAVE ALREADY SEEN that things we take for granted, such as book shelves with books standing upright and with their spine facing outwards, in fact took a couple of hundred years after printing began to become common practice. Similarly, we go to a modern bookshop and expect the title page to tell us the author and title of a book and details of the publisher, place and date of publication.

However, the title page also had a slow and interesting evolution. Manuscript books did not have one and it took until the 1530s, some seventy-five years after printing was introduced, for every printed book to have a title page.

Why did manuscript books not have title pages?

The process of acquiring a manuscript book was very different from buying a printed book. Manuscript books were usually made by a scribe on commission for a known purchaser. The purchaser would then have the completed book bound and added to his library. It would have been a local transaction in most cases and the manuscript would be delivered on completion without the need for any transportation or storage.

Manuscripts would normally begin with the title of the book written on the first page in red, to be followed immediately beneath by the first line of the text in black. The title heading is known as an incipit (which translates as "here begins"). So a separate title page was not customary, especially as the book's title would be written on the parchment or wooden outer cover.

Normal practice was that the scribe, or more often the artist, responsible for the brightly coloured initial letters and borders, would sign at the back of the book to say who they were and what book had been copied. This is similar to an artist signing a painting or a craftsmen putting a mark on a piece of silver or pottery.

Manuscript books did sometimes have ornamental pages at the beginning if they were being made as a special presentation. These are more typical in later books from 1500.

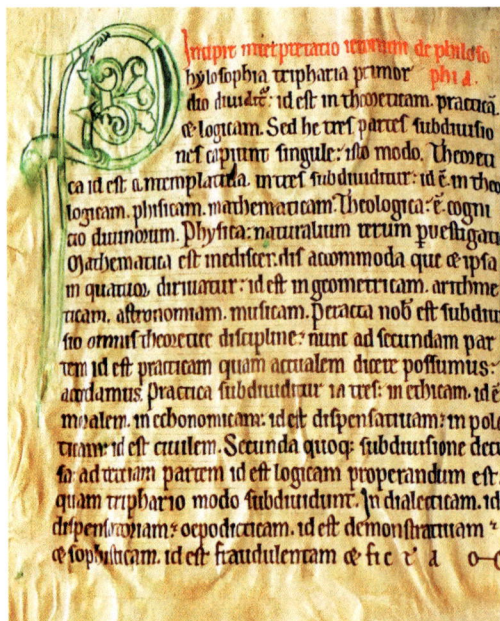

Illustration of a manuscript 'incipit' from our copy of the works of Hugo Floriacensis believed to be written in the twelfth century at the Cistercian monastery at Garendon in Leicestershire.

So title pages began with printed books?

The title page in printed books had a slow evolution. The earliest printed books from 1455 did not have one. Again, copying the practice with manuscript books, the first page of text might have a brief note of author and title at the top of the page before the text began.

Some, but not all, also copied the practice of the makers of manuscript books and put a note at the end of the book which may have included any or all of the author, title, name of the printer, and the date and place of publication. This was called a COLOPHON.

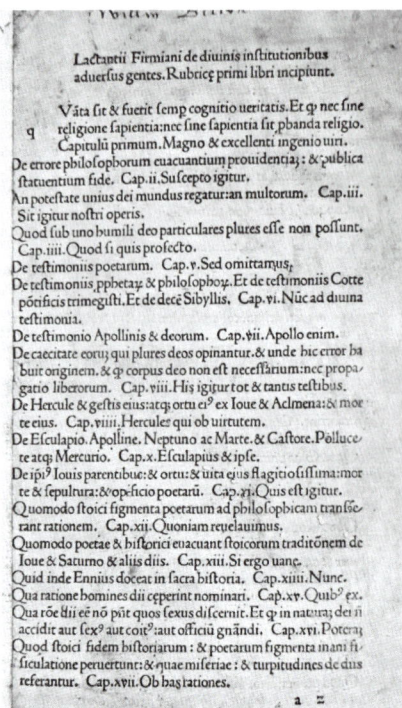

Example of a printed book with no title page but early 'incipit'. This is from Lactantius *De Divinus Institutionibus Adversus*, printed in Venice in 1478 by Johannes de Colonia, which is in the Bath Abbey collection.

Advertising the name of the printer was good practice as readers were often faced with pirated or poor quality imitations of books. Seeing the name of a scholar printer indicated a book that was carefully edited and known to be made from reliable manuscripts. Many of these printers also began to add an illustrated mark or device as a sort of trademark to make their books easier to recognise. We will look at these devices in the next chapter as they are addictively fascinating.

A good example of such an early and simple colophon is from our copy of Pliny the Elder's *Natural History* printed by Nicholas Jenson in Venice in 1472:

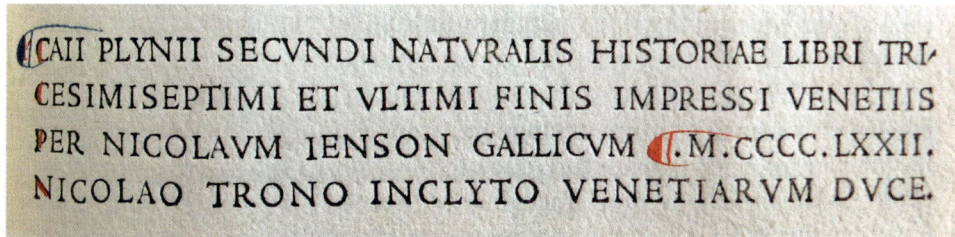

However, many early printed books had no details of the printer, date or place and have had to be identified in other ways such as examining the source of the paper, the type of font used by the printer, the signature of the illuminator of the initial capitals and borders, or the pastedowns in the binding.

Why were title pages thought to be useful?

Printers had worked out that sending books unbound to save money on transport, could often mean that the first printed page would be damaged on arrival. This led to a blank page being used as a form of wrapper. Also, booksellers would often store printed books folded but unbound for a few years before selling them to a customer. Binding in advance made no sense as it tied up capital with no guarantee of selling the stock. It eventually seemed useful to put a brief title on this blank page to help identify which book was which on their storeroom shelves. This also stopped the time wasting of having to hunt the colophon at the back which was not always in an obvious place. Such rudimentary title pages would have one or two words of the title in fairly small letters on a blank page and were called LABEL TITLES. A good example can be found on one of our incunabula, the legal text of Bartolus de Saxoferrata printed by Baptista de Tortis in Venice in 1499 [*right*].

Research on Baptista's publications has shown that between 1481-92 he only used blank white sheets for title pages, but from 1493-1500 all but one of his twenty-seven books had a brief title page as illustrated.

What information was on these early title pages?

Label titles were mere finding tools and were a brief version of the title. The main details about the book were still found in the colophon which was found near the back of the book. However, at some point, the more enterprising bookseller/printers worked out that a title page could also be used as a marketing tool.

Unlike modern books with their dust jackets or brightly coloured paperback covers filled with information to attract the buyer, early books had at best a plain cover or were sold unbound. The only information about the book was on the title page. Moving this on from being a protective sheet and finding tool to a more attractive and informative marketing device was a process that really began in about 1500. Printers would frequently make additional copies of title pages which could be displayed or circulated to advertise their books. Design of the title page was normally the responsibility of the printer and not the author (if he was alive). And so gradually the information moved from the colophon at the back to the title page and some ornamentation was introduced. A character in a Fielding novel proclaimed that *"A title page is to a book what a fine neck is to a woman, and therefore ought to be the most regarded as it is the part which is to be viewed before the Purchase"*.

The colophon did not die out and was frequently retained until

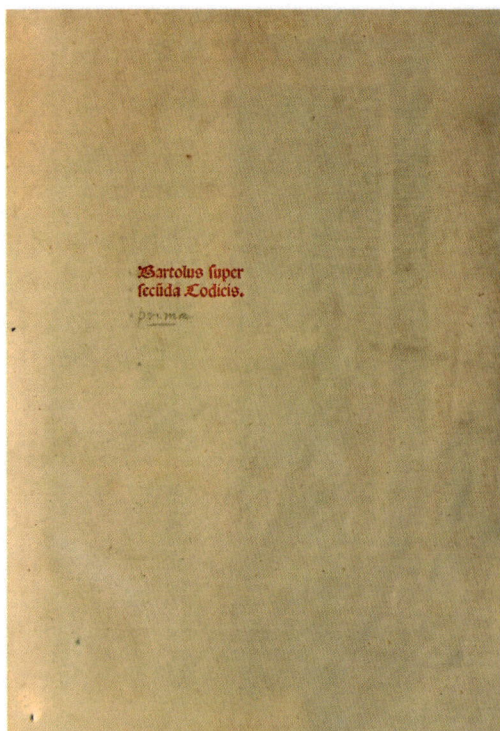

about 1600. Its disappearance paralleled the sublimation of the scholar printer to the commercial interests of the publisher.

It is estimated that only 1% of books printed between 1455 and 1484 had a title page but this had risen to 40% between 1485 and 1500. By 1530 it was uncommon for a book not to have one.

How did the design of title pages evolve?

The simple label title became a bit more elaborate:

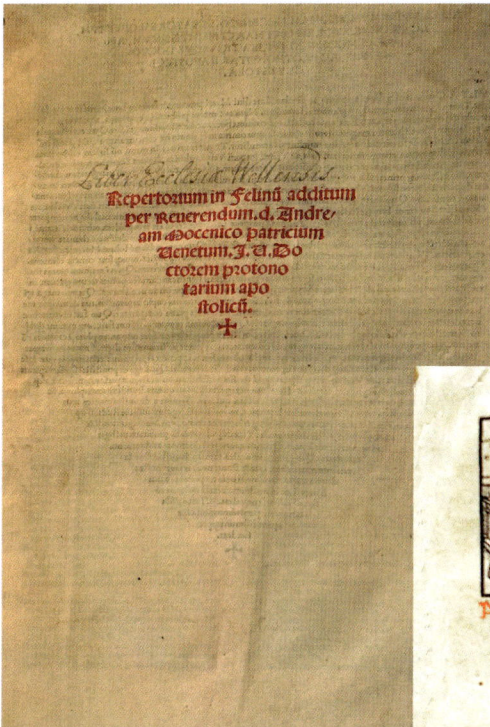

[*left*] The 'half diamond' title page from Andeas Mocenigo's *Repertorium in Felinum* printed in Venice in 1507 by Giovanni and Gregorio de Gregori.

Woodcuts were introduced by some printers at about this time:

[*right*] Woodcut used on a title page from Joannes Andreae *Mercuriales Domini* printed in Lyons in 1510 by Joannem de la Place.

Title pages with frames became popular in the first half of the sixteenth century:

This example, [*below left*] is the works of Dionysius the Carthusian, printed in Cologne in 1533 by John Soteris.

A second example [*below right*] is from the collected works of Martin Luther in seven volumes printed in Wittemberg in 1558 by Thomas Klug: [*See also further illustrations of framed title pages: in Chapter Six, the Hans Holbein frame; and in Chapter Seventeen the 1552 Book of Common Prayer.*]

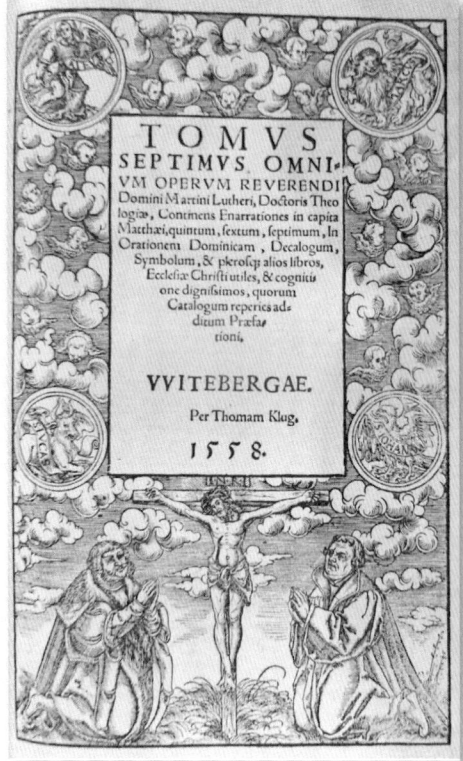

The Baroque period led to elaborate engravings that many purists feel were self-indulgent, pompous and pretentious. By this time, copper engraving had taken over from woodcuts. The emblematic title-pages described in the book by Corbett and Lightbown, of which the *Poly-Olbion* is a good example, did see a swing towards the author influencing the design of the title page rather than the printer.

The symbols used were conceits of the author using allegory and imagery from ancient myth and religion, and were intended to be obscure except for his like-minded friends.

Title page of Michael Drayton's *Poly-Olbion,*
designed by William Hole and printed in 1612.

A continental example is the works of Sulpicus Severus, printed by Elzevir in Amsterdam, 1665 [*right*]: [*See also in Chapter One: the illustration of the title page of Colom's book of sea charts, 1632; and in Chapter Eleven the title page of Walton's* Polyglot Bible *of 1657*].

In the late seventeenth century and eighteenth century, title pages became very verbose in their attempts to attract people to purchase the book. These are known as 'bill of fare' title pages as they attempt to comprehensively account for the contents. Further examples can be seen in Chapter Eleven, ie: Minsheu's *Ductor in Linguas* and Castell's *Lexicon Heptaglotton*. This trend came to an end with the improvement in bibliographical publications and book review journals.

The late eighteenth century brought the neo-classic period exemplifying simplicity of design and vitality of spirit. The mood was captured in England with the printing of John Baskerville (1706-75) and in Italy with Giambattista Bodoni (1740-1813). Here there was subtlety in exact spacing and the use of a limited range of type sizes and a more strictly limited range of type faces to achieve perfect proportion.

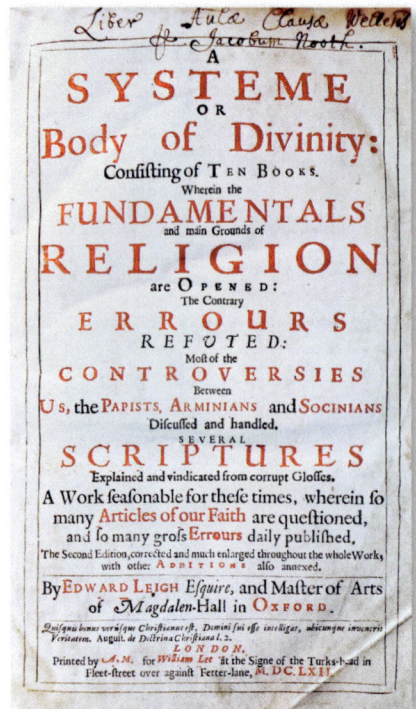

Example of a 'bill of fare' title page, printed in London in 1657.

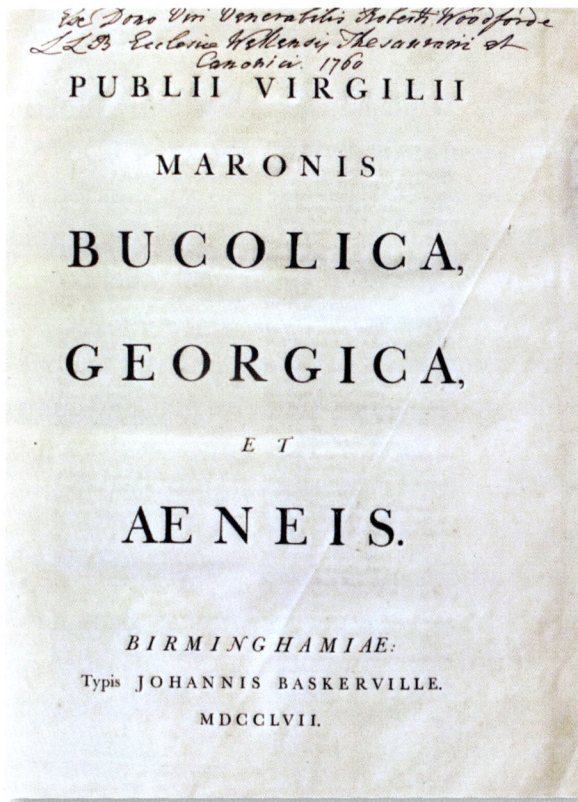

Baskerville's printing of Virgil in 1757.

How reliable was the information on title pages?

Bibliographers delight in finding false imprints and a reviewer of books in the Monthly Review of 1772 declared that *"It is a fundamental article in the creed of a Reviewer, that no trust is to be put in title pages"*. A number of Shakespeare's plays were found to have INCORRECT DATES when watermarks and other evidence was examined. FALSE LOCATIONS for the place of printing were also not uncommon. These came about more frequently with pirated copies of books such as the Bible. Because of the monopoly of printing of bibles in England granted by the Crown which supposedly guaranteed the quality of the product, prices were quite high. Dutch printers would print copies much more cheaply and export them to England having put London as the city of printing in order to fool the authorities and to reassure the purchaser. And in the early days of the Reformation, Reformed printers on the continent would locate themselves in "Utopia" or even "Rome, at St. Peter's court".

Despite the best efforts of the Stationers' Company and their fearsome powers of enforcement [*see Chapter Nineteen*], circulation of imported books that were illegal copies was fairly widespread. Piracy of books was also common in Ireland as the 1709 Copyright Act did not extend there until 1800, and booksellers were often reluctant to sell books to Ireland for fear that they would be copied and sold more cheaply. The Stationers imposed harsh fines on booksellers found with pirated books but it was not unknown for them to release the confiscated books in order to then fine another set of booksellers and so double their money.

Unscrupulous booksellers would also make attractive their old and unsold stock by having a NEW TITLE PAGE PRINTED with a different author, title and date to replace the original, easily done when books were sold unbound.

Printing an author's manuscript WITHOUT PERMISSION was also common. A famous example is Thomas Browne's *Religio Medici* which he had never intended for publication, but when an unauthorised printed copy appeared in 1642, he felt obliged to issue a corrected version the following year and our copy notes the indignation.

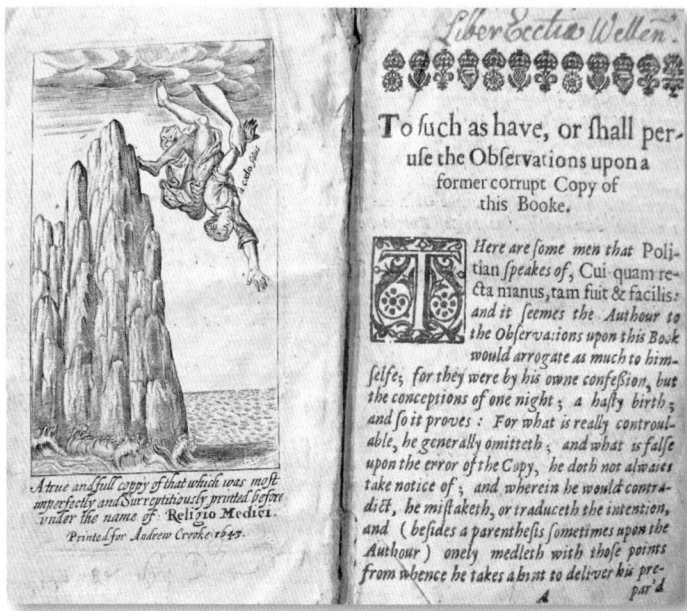

The opening pages of Thomas Browne's "authorised version"
of his *Religio Medici*, printed in 1643.

In troubled times anonymity led to the absence of an author's name. One such book is Thomas Harrington's *Common-Wealth of Oceana* published in 1656 during Cromwell's Protectorate. It is a book outlining a utopian republic and was seized from the press but eventually published with a dedication to Cromwell following intercession through his daughter. The book was later influential in the drafting of the American Constitution.

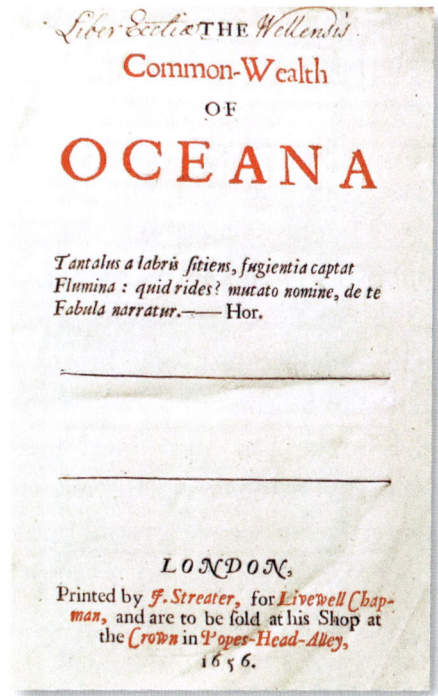

Title page of Harrington's
The Common-Wealth of Oceana, printed in 1656.

Early title pages can be confusing in that they say printed by but sold for someone else at a certain bookshop?

In the early days of printing, the roles of publisher, printer and distributor were still being worked out and this meant title pages were not as clear as those found today. Common formulations were:

1] *Imprinted at London in Fleet streate, at the signe of the Oliphante, by Henry Wykes. Anno 1566.*

2] *Printed by Edw. Griffin, for Iohn Gwillim, and are to be sold at his shop in Britaines-Burse. 1615.*

3] *Printed by H. Lownes, and are to be sold by Cuthbert Wright in S. Bartholomews, neer the entrance into the Hospital. 1626.*

4] *Printed at London by A. I. for Thomas Gubbins and are to be sold by Iohn Busbie, 1592*

Printers like Caxton were also publishers, which meant they were enterprising enough to find a text they thought would sell and would negotiate with the author if still alive, took responsibility for editing the text, and also took the financial risk of printing and selling the book. Their imprints would be like the first example above.

In the second example, it would look that John Gwillim was the publisher who had the 'copyright', but would have contracted Griffin to print the book. However, printers could often obtain manuscripts and not want the task of editing them. In which case, Gwillim would be asked to be the publisher on the condition that Griffin printed and sold the book. The third and fourth examples are further permutations whereby publisher/printers would prefer to focus on their area of expertise and leave a retail bookseller to sell their publications. It should be noted that printed or imprinted often means published. Although there is often some lack of clarity with early printed books about the various responsibilities, the role of author and publisher are more important than the printer, and the publisher's name should be the one on the Stationers' register [*see Chapter Nineteen*].

What is the difference between a title page and a frontispiece?

A distinctive feature of a title page is that it must be separate from the first page of the text of the book. If the title page was illustrated it might have been called a frontispiece, and in the period of the books in the Chained Library, up to 1800, the two terms are to some extent interchangeable. On a modern book, the frontispiece is an illustrated page facing the title page.

WHERE CAN I READ MORE ABOUT THIS?

BENNETT, H. S. – *English Books and Readers, Vol II, 1558-1603* –
Cambridge University Press [CUP], 1965

CAMBRIDGE HISTORY OF THE BOOK IN BRITAIN, Vols. IV and V –
CUP, 2002 and 2009

COLE, GAROLD – *The Historical Development of the Title Page* –
Journal of Library History, Vol.6, No.4, Oct. 1971, pp.303-16

CORBETT, MARGERY and LIGHTBROWN, R. W. – *The Comely Frontispiece:
the emblematic title-page in England 1550-1660* – Routledge, 1979
(In the Reading Room at 096)

DE VINNE, THEODORE – *A Treatise on Title-Pages* – Century NY, 1902

SHAABER, M. A. – *The meaning of the imprint in early printed books* –
Library, XXIV, 4, 1944, pp.120-141

SHEVLIN, ELEANOR – *To reconcile book and title, and make 'em kin to one
another: the evolution of the title's contractual functions* – Book History,
Vol.2.1, 1999, pp.42-77

SMITH, MARGARET – *The Title-Page: its early development 1460-1510* –
British Library, 2000 (in the Reading Room at 094)

CHAPTER EIGHT

Printers' Marks

What are printers' marks?

IN THE EARLY DAYS OF PRINTING, from 1455-1600, printers would often have a decorative trademark or logo printed on the title page or colophon at the back of the book to help identify their work. The design would be cut in wood or engraved on metal. It could include the printer's initials, often with a simple design or a quite elaborate picture with symbols or plays on the printer's name like a bishop's rebus. The use of such a mark or device was to make it easier for buyers to detect a pirated copy of their work as it was harder to forge a printers' mark than to simply reprint their work. A common mark, especially in Italy, involved the orb and cross with the printer's initials. The mark below of Baptista de Tortis is a good example. A later mark commonly involved the figure 4 which was in general use as a trade mark by printers and bookbinders and other guilds of craftsmen. The mark of Claude Chevallon illustrated below shows this symbol and a further example is the mark of the Cambridge binder, Nicholas Spierinck, which is shown in Chapter Eighteen.

Do all of our early books have printers' marks?

Most of our early books were printed on the Continent as the bulk of them are in Latin or even Greek, and printing in Britain concentrated on production of books in English. Foreign printers varied in their adoption of marks, some having none and others using several. And their practice varied over time.

A good example is our set of Aristotle's work printed in Greek between 1495-8 by the great Venetian publisher ALDUS MANUTIUS (1449-1515).

His famous mark was a dolphin and anchor, often with the motto *Festina lente,* or make haste slowly.

But this was only introduced in 1502 and so does not appear in this set of volumes. Aldus is famed as one of the great Humanist publishers who printed books almost exclusively in Greek in the early days and then concentrated on Roman writers. He introduced Italic type and also made popular the octavo, or pocket sized, copies of the classics in his Aldine editions.

The mark of Aldus Manutius from 1502

Which other famous printers are represented in the collection?

The great Humanist, Desiderius Erasmus (1466-1536) worked closely with some of the early printers as a proof-reader and to supervise printing of his own books. He worked with Aldus but preferred to have his own books printed in Basle at the workshop of JOHANN FROBEN (1460-1527). Erasmus lived in the house of Froben for some time and helped supervise the printing of many of the classical editions of the works of Jerome, Cyprian, etc.

Froben published Erasmus's translation of the New Testament in Greek in 1516, one of the key books that influenced the Protestant Reformation. Our copy of this book is the 1539 edition.

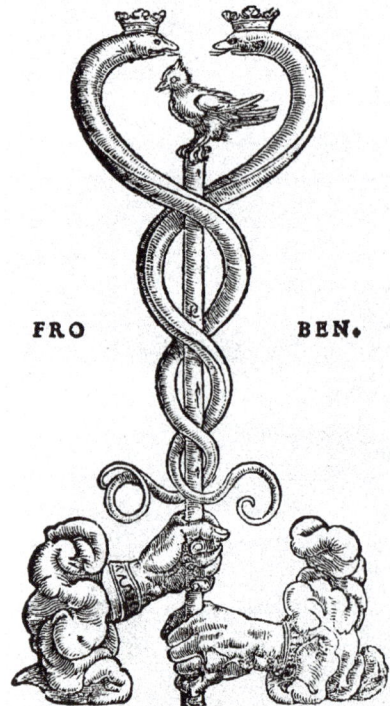

Another Basle printer was JOHANNES OPORINUS (1507-68) and we have several

The mark of Froben

of his works including the famous book of human anatomy by Andreas Vesalius, *De Humani Corporis Fabrica,* the second edition of 1555.

Oporinus had worked for Froben and was also a lecturer in Greek at the university in Basle. He then devoted himself full time to printing and produced a variety of works of church history and a translation of the Koran. His mark showed the mythological lyre player Arion of Lesbos standing on a dolphin.

The ESTIENNE FAMILY were scholar printers in Paris and Geneva. The first of the family was Henri Estienne (1470-1520) who was fastidious and the first printer to issue errata sheets should a mistake escape the proof-reader. His mark was of a type that framed early title pages:

The mark of Oporinus in our copy of Vesalius

The olive tree with falling branch.
Mark of Robert Estienne.

Mark of Henri Estienne framing a title page

He had three sons. Robert Estienne, known as Robertus Stephanus in Latin, eventually moved to Geneva to escape religious persecution and adopted the olive tree with an entwined serpent as his mark with the motto *Noli altum sapere, sed time* (Do not be arrogant but fear). He printed mainly classical texts and grammars but also bibles and was the first to divide the New Testament into verses.

Robert Estienne had three sons too and they all became printers working in either Paris or Geneva.

CHRISTOPHER PLANTIN (1520-89) was born in France and started work as a bookbinder. He moved to Antwerp and then began a prolific career as a printer. Many of his publications were Catholic texts and he is best known for the eight-volume Polyglot Bible of 1569-73 that was printed at the request and with the assistance of the King of Spain. We have a copy in the library shelved next to the Walton Polyglot of 1657. His printer's mark has the motto *Labore et Constantia* (Energy and persistence) which

Christopher Plantin's mark with a compass

surrounds the symbol of a compass inscribing a circle held by a hand extending from a bank of clouds. At one time, Plantin had twenty printing presses in his workshop. The workshop has been preserved as the Plantin-Moretus Museum, which houses the two oldest surviving printing presses in the world.

The library also has books with marks from lesser known printers that are still of interest:

SIMON BEVILAQUA printed in Venice from about 1485-1512, and there is a Bible of his printed in 1498 in the Bath Abbey collection.

[*right*] The mark of Simon Bevilaqua

We have four very large books of law printed in Venice in 1499 and 1500 so qualifying as incunabula. These were printed by BAPTISTA DE TORTIS who specialised in law publications from about 1481-1500. His mark of the orb and cross is very typical of early Italian printers who adopted this logo but added their own initials. This is one of the few in colour. (It is interesting that all OREO biscuits have the same *globus cruciger*. This is because in 1900 the company chairman of what was to become Nabisco, Adolphus Green, who was a bibliophile, was looking for a logo and remembered this design from his book collection).

[*right*] The orb and cross mark of Baptista de Tortis

A personal favourite is the mark of JOSSE BADIUS (1462-1535) who printed in Paris [*below*]. We have three of his books all with slightly

Mark of Josse Badius
(note the press braced against the ceiling)

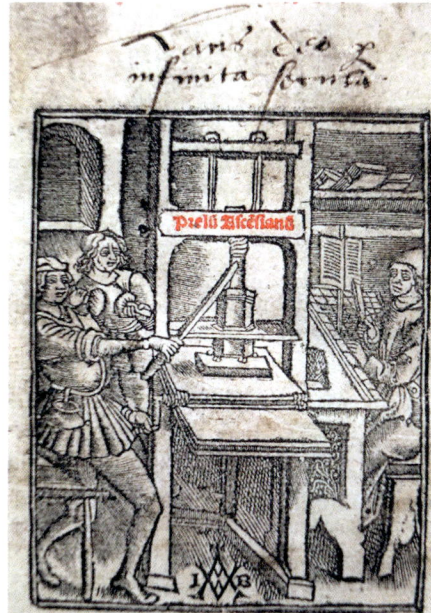

A later mark of Josse Badius

differing versions of the mark with an early printing press. He specialised in printing Roman classics from 1503 until his death and Erasmus worked with him on his earlier publications.

A printer of the classics and religious books was JEREMIE DES PLANCHES in Geneva in the late sixteenth century. We have the four volumes of his printing of the works of Cicero dating from 1584.

THOMAS GUARINUM was printing in Basle in the late sixteenth century and adopted a palm tree for his mark and we have a book of his printed in 1573. [*left*]

Mark of Jeremie des Planches

Mark of Claude Chevallon

CLAUDE CHEVALLON (1479-1537) printed in Paris and is best known by a mark with two horses, cheval being a horse in French, so making it like a bishop's rebus. But when he married the widow of Berthold Rembolt who printed in Strasbourg, he combined his mark with that of Rembolt which had a symbol for salvation, two lions and a vine tree with the mysterious figure 4.

HENRICUS PETRUS printed in Basle from 1523-78 and adopted a mark [*right*] showing Thor's hammer held by a hand issuing from the cloud striking fire on a rock, while a head, symbolising wind, blows upon it.

Mark of Henricus Petrus

ROBERT HERVAGIUM was another Basle printer, who knew Erasmus, and his mark [*left*] is taken from the Bible concordance that he printed in 1553.

Yet another Basle printer was **JOHANN BEBEL** who was a journeyman with Froben until he set up his own press in 1524.

[*left*] Mark of Johann Bebel

HIERONYMUS COMMELINI in Heidelberg and his mark of a naked lady holding a book in one hand and the sun in the other representing Truth, appears in a book published in 1594. [*right*]

Basle printers would often share risk by printing major works together, and this mark of a basilisk bearing the coat of arms of the City of Basle was used from 1511 by **JOHANN AMERBACH**, **FROBEN** and **HENRICUS PETRUS** on a printing of the works of St. Anthony.

Mark of Jan Januszowski

Mark of Amerbach, Froben and Petrus

One of our few books published in Poland is a work by the Polish Reformation theologian, Stanislaus Sokolowski, who was chaplain to the King of Poland. This is the printer's mark of **JAN JANUSZOWSKI** who was so highly regarded that he was known as the "Polish Plantin".

WHERE CAN I READ MORE ABOUT THIS?

DAVIES, HUGH – *Devices of the Early Printers 1457-1560* – Dawsons, 1935

ROBERTS, WILLIAM – *Printers' Marks: a chapter in the history of typography* – Bell, 1893 and available on the Internet at: http://www.gutenberg.org/files/25663/25663-h/25663-h.htm

VICTORIA AND ALBERT MUSEUM – *Printers' Marks* – 1962

WINGER, HOWARD – *Printers' Marks and Devices* – Caxton Club, Chicago, 1976

CHAPTER NINE

Illustrating the Printed Book

Were early printed books illustrated?

AS WE SAW in Chapter Five, the earliest printed books from 1455 did their best to look like manuscript books and were often decorated by the same artists who produced manuscript illustration. However, illustration of this sort was expensive and meant that such books were principally bought by the more affluent. The effect of printing was to 'democratise' books and make them far more affordable for ordinary people, or at least those with enough education to be able to read.

Printers soon realised that there would not be enough illustrators to cope with the output of printing and they looked to substitute the decorative painting by woodcut capitals, pictures and patterns that could be printed on the page, usually in black but sometimes in red.

Why were woodcuts chosen?

Germany in the 1400s had become a centre for woodcut illustration. Playing cards were made from woodcuts as also devotional prints of saints and similar figures that pilgrims would buy and use to decorate their homes. Prior to printing with moveable type, 'block books' were produced which were compilations of pages of illustration and also the text printed from carved wooden blocks. A popular block book was the *Biblia Pauperum* (the Pauper's Bible) which attempted to tell stories from the Bible from illustrations [*see overleaf*]. This allowed people to have religious depictions in their own homes to complement and personalise what they had seen on stained glass in churches.

Biblia Pauperum

The principal advantage of a woodcut is that it allows for easy replication of the image. Woodcuts would eventually crack or wear out but it was a much quicker and cheaper task to replace them than for an artist to make hundreds of individual paintings.

How are woodcuts made?

A hardwood such as box, cherry, apple or pear would normally be chosen and then a picture sketched out on its smoothed surface. The wood would then be gouged away using chisels and specialist tools such as burins so that just the fine lines of the required design remained at the original surface level. The woodcut, being in relief just as the type in a printing press, could then be inserted in to the laid out text and inked in the same way as the type ready to be pressed on paper. Simple rubber stamps pressed on an inkpad work on the same principle. Wood engraving is much the same but is usually finer in detail. The difference is that a woodcut is made from the side grain, or plankwise, whereas wood engraving is carved on the end grain.

Making a woodcut
Illustration courtesy of Tugboat Printshop,
http://www.featherofme.com/tugboat-printshop-intricate-woodcut-prints/

70

What sort of woodcuts are found in early printed books?

The most common woodcuts are INITIAL CAPITAL LETTERS used principally for decoration. Many printers would acquire sets of capitals which would travel with them should they move to a new city. These replaced the hand painted capitals of the illuminated manuscript.

CRUDE PICTURES OF CHARACTERS portrayed in the text are also found in the earliest books such as the pilgrims in Chaucer's *Canterbury Tales*:

Such books were intended to edify a huge public that could hardly read, to explain the text through the medium of pictures, to make real and comprehensible the different episodes in the life of Christ, the prophets and the saints, and to make mythical and legendary personalities familiar to the readers of that age. Book illustration answered a

Woodcut from the Knight's Tale in the Bath Abbey's copy of Chaucer from 1561.

practical need rather than an artistic need: to make graphic and visible what people of the time constantly heard evoked. There is no subtle variation of light and shade, or of tone; just a few simple figures cut with clear and obvious features.

The Renaissance tended to bring to an end these woodcuts in the works of mainstream publishers as the Humanists scorned the idea of illustrations for a public too ignorant to be able to comprehend text without the aid of pictures. They were relegated to inferior quality printers along the lines of comic books today.

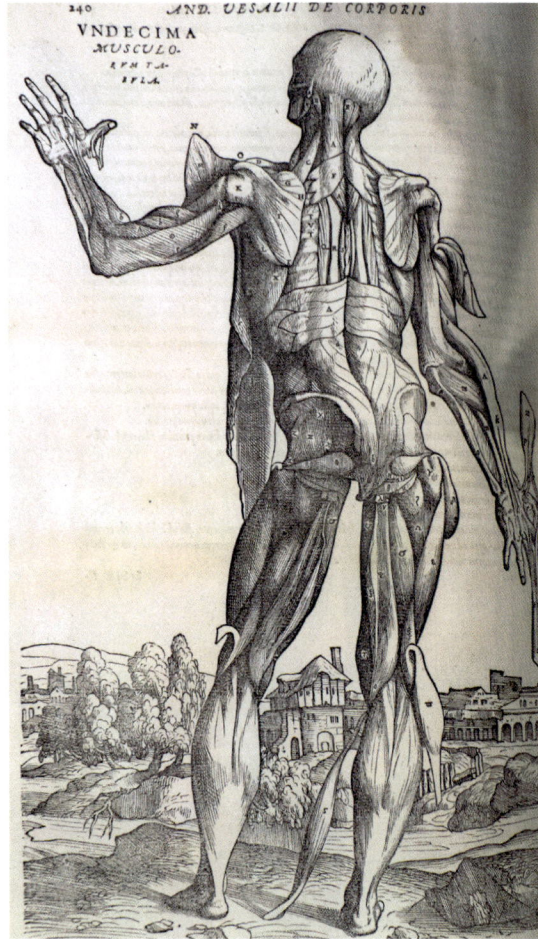

From Vesalius's *De Humani Corporis Fabrica*, printed by Oporinus in 1555.

However, in the sixteenth century especially, we see woodcuts used to ILLUSTRATE SCIENTIFIC TEXTS and other such books where illustration would genuinely help the understanding of the reader. One of the finest examples is the first real book of human anatomy by the great Vesalius, first printed in 1543. Woodcuts could allow fine detail if they were large enough and these plates are folio size and are believed to have been made by a pupil of Titian named Jan van Calcar. We are extremely fortunate to have the second edition of 1555 in the Chained Library as this is one of the great books of the Renaissance and influenced early scientists who went on to found The Royal Society a hundred years later. A point often made to visitors is that, if you could make a drawing like this by hand on parchment, how many could you make in a week and how accurate would each one be? Whereas a detailed woodcut and a printing press makes dissemination of scientific information possible.

When did copper engraving take over from woodcuts?

Engraving or etching on metal, usually copper, was known from at least the fifteenth century. Suits of armour were engraved for the richer patrons and the work had usually been done by gold and silversmiths. After printing began, artists realised that they could make designs on metal which could then be printed on paper. The first copper engraved book printed in England dates from 1540 and the technique allowed more faithful rendering of light and shade and lines of greater subtlety. The problem was that engraving is an intaglio process whereby the design that you need printed is incised in the metal. Because it is incised, it cannot be printed alongside the metal type of text in the same way as the relief of a woodcut can be printed. Copper engraving requires a separate press. The smooth copper plate is inked so that the ink remains in the incised design but the smooth surfaces are wiped clean. The separate press then squeezes damp paper on to the inked engraving so that the ink is transferred to the paper.

Etching on metal is similar to engraving in the way it is printed but the process differs. Here the metal plate is covered in wax and the design carved on the wax. The copper is then put in a solution of acid so that the acid cuts into the design area where the wax has been removed. After the acid has done its work, the wax is wiped off and the plate is inked in the same way as with an engraved plate ready for printing. Many designs use a combination of etching and engraving so that large areas can be prepared by etching and then only the fine lines added with an engraving tool.

The simplicity for the printer of a woodcut meant that they persisted until the late sixteenth century. However, copper engraving was relatively simple to use if whole pages were reproduced and then inserted along with printed pages at the binding stage. This simplified their use and meant usually better quality reproductions. Copper engraving was more difficult if you wanted to print text and have a copper engraved illustration on the same page as it meant having to put the same page through the press twice. Copper engraving became more popular in the latter half of the sixteenth century and largely replaced woodcuts when printers had worked out how best to use them. Its primacy over wood lasted for some 200 years. Wood engraving became popular again in the late eighteenth century when Thomas Bewick (1753-1828) popularised it with his drawings of wildlife and the countryside. But we see copper engraving continuing to illustrate books of travel, architecture, history etc. way beyond the last book added to the Chained Library.

Were book illustrations important as an art form?

Some illustrations did achieve fame. The most obvious example is the engraving by William Marshall from Charles the First's *Eikon Basilike* which we have in the Chained Library. This book, published days after Charles's execution in 1649, portrayed him as a martyr. The illustration became a rallying tool for the Royalists and was reproduced endlessly in pamphlets and on objects such as snuff boxes. It was so popular that Marshall had to re-engrave it eight times.

Some famous artists also illustrated books. Albrecht Durer's wood engravings in the fifteenth century were popular in printed books. We have seen in Chapter Six that Hans Holbein assisted Cuthbert Tunstall with a frontispiece for his *De Arte Supputandi* of 1522. Another example in the library is the illustrations of Peter Paul Rubens (1577-1640) in a book on optics written by the Belgian Jesuit Francois de Aguilon in 1613 entitled *Opticorum Libri Sex*.

Eikon Basilike frontispiece

An engraving from *Opticorum Libri Sex*, from Rubens's painting.

Rubens made the paintings as he was a friend of the printer Jan Moretus, son-in-law of Christopher Plantin, and because he was interested as an artist in the subject. Although he painted the pictures, another artist would have made the copper engraving.

How were maps reproduced in atlases?

The first recognised atlas is the one by Abraham Ortelius who was Dutch and a friend of Mercator. This was first published in 1570 but later enlarged and we have the English translated edition of 1606. The maps are all copper engraved and then hand coloured. The addition of colour to a map was typically done for one of two reasons. The first was to make the map easier to use, by delineating borders, highlighting cities, or identifying regions or topographical features. The second reason for colouring a map was to embellish the image and make it more attractive. Beginning in the latter part of the sixteenth century, virtually all of the most famous atlases (Ortelius, Mercator, Hondius, Blaeu, Jansson, Visscher, De Wit, etc.) were offered either coloured or uncoloured by the original publishers. Over time, some of the uncoloured examples were coloured at a later date. We think our copy was coloured at the time of publication.

An engraving of a map of Iceland [detail], from the 1606 edition of the Ortelius atlas.

What other techniques have been used to illustrate books?

Aquatints were a refinement of copper engraving allowing subtler forms of shading and became popular from the 1790s to the 1830s. Steel engraving began to take over from copper as it was more hard wearing in the 1820s. The first lithographed book in England was published in 1803. The beginnings of photogravure were in 1826 and the first book relief half-tone was in 1854. The first book using photographs was Henry Fox Talbot's *The Pencil of Nature* serialised between 1844-6. As such, all of these came after the books in the Chained Library which were published before 1800.

WHERE CAN I READ MORE ABOUT THIS?

DRIVER, MARTHA – *The Image in Print: book illustration in late medieval England* – British Library, 2004

FEBVRE, LUCIEN and MARTIN, H. J. – *The Coming of the Book* – Verso, 1976

SUAREZ, MICHAEL and WOUDHUYSEN, H. – *The Book: a Global History* – Oxford University Press, 2013

CHAPTER TEN

The Transition from Manuscript to Print

How quickly did print take over from manuscript book production?

THERE WAS NO SUDDEN END to the production of manuscript books. Their production could still be traced as late as about 1700. Just as electronic and printed books co-exist today, the transition was slow as the pace of life was much slower in the Early Modern period and people tend to be conservative by nature. Even in our own library, the Hailes Psalter was written in 1514 whereas the Nicholas Jenson printing of Pliny the Elder's *Natural History* was forty years earlier in 1472.

Why did manuscript books persist?

There were many reasons:

ℰ Some authors preferred to CONTROL THE CIRCULATION of their writing which could be done better with hand written and distributed books. Manuscript books were regarded as more intimate and also had an aura of forbidden knowledge. John Donne (1572-1631) is a classic example as he was aware that his metaphysical love poems could be damaging to his reputation in certain circles so they were only ever in manuscript until published after his death. (We have a first edition of the 1633 printing of the poems in the library.) However, when he was elevated to be the Dean of St. Paul's cathedral, he was pleased to have his sermons printed and distributed as widely as possible.

Early scientists at the time of the founding of The Royal Society would also send their initial work in manuscript to a select group of peers for approval before considering printing.

🐿 The sixteenth and seventeenth centuries were DANGEROUS TIMES. Many religious and political writings could easily fall foul of the authorities and so printers may well refuse to publish books that could cause them to be fined or worse. We only have to remember in recent times the *samizdat* circulation of hand-written works by dissident authors such as Solzhenitsyn in Soviet Russia to realise the fear of repression. Although Boris Pasternak was awarded the Nobel Prize for Literature in 1958 for *Dr. Zhivago*, it had

William Tyndale being executed for translating and publishing the Bible into English, 1536.

only circulated in manuscript in Russia until serialised in 1988.

🐿 Books that might have a LIMITED AUDIENCE could often be copied more cheaply by a scribe than risking the cost of setting the text in print to produce more copies than could be economically sold. Poetry books today struggle to find a commercial publisher.

🐿 Women writers had to overcome prejudice and often resorted to circulation in manuscript

🐿 People living far from London, where printing was concentrated, could also choose manuscript

🐿 Some people just preferred the often more BEAUTIFULLY DECORATED manuscript books and had the money to indulge their tastes.

Why did print succeed?

Obviously, as we have already discussed in Chapter Five, the speed of production and lower cost of printed books made them more accessible and some ten million books, pamphlets and broadsides had appeared before 1500.

But many people saw them as more authoritative than manuscripts, especially from a reputable publisher. Manuscripts were copied one by one and sometimes the versions that they were copied from were inaccurate or the scribe made mistakes. Printed books were never perfect either, but many saw them as better and we have plenty of evidence of college libraries and even monasteries throwing out their old manuscripts when a printed version was purchased. Some of the Benedictine monasteries even established their own printing presses. Many of us can recall throwing out vinyl records in favour of cassettes and CDs as they did not have clicks and scratches and took up less space.

Some early printed books look as if they copied manuscripts in their design?

This was quite deliberate. Printers knew that they were trying to sell people books that were unlike the manuscript books that had been around for hundreds of years and so they went out of their way to make the transition as painless as possible. We have some good examples in the library:

- The FONT DESIGN for early printed books very much copied the manuscript styles preferred by scribes.
- Although small size manuscript books were not uncommon, eg: the Paris bibles, most were in the larger folio size and early printed books were also this large size until the early 1500s.
- Printers would leave the initial capital letters of a paragraph blank to be coloured by hand to make them look more like a manuscript. The printer would add a small initial letter in the space to act as a guide to the rubricator
- Paragraph marks were used in manuscripts to guide the reader that there was a break. This was later done in printed books by changing the layout of the page, but in the days when parchment and paper were expensive, it took less space to add a paragraph mark [*right*]. These have been hand coloured in red in Thomas Cranmer's copy of the works of St. John of Damascus, printed in 1512.

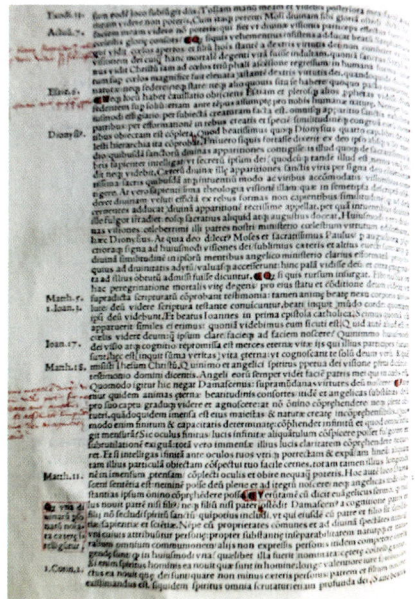

🙋 Scribes had not put a TITLE PAGE at the front of a manuscript but noted briefly at the end what the work was and sometimes who had written it. Early printers did the same, the note at the end being called a colophon as we have seen in Chapter Seven which looked at the evolution of title pages.

🙋 Scribes had not used PAGE NUMBERS and printers rarely used them before 1500. We have some good examples of experimenting with page numbers, eg: the Aldus Manutius five volume set of Aristotle's work printed from 1495-8 has a page number only on the right hand page. The need for page numbers became more apparent when indexes were added at the back of books after about 1525. Before that, a contents list was sometimes placed at the front of the book.

🙋 Some of our early printed books have CLASPS on the covers. These were needed with manuscript books made of parchment so that there was a pressure to stop the skin becoming wavy in damp conditions. Paper does not do this and so clasps were really unnecessary, but because people were used to having clasps on their books, they persisted. [*See also Chapter Eighteen on Bookbinding*].

Woodcut showing clasped books, most probably manuscript, from our copy of the works of Denis the Carthusian (1402-71) printed in Cologne in 1532.

WHERE CAN I READ MORE ABOUT THIS?

BLAND, MARK – *A Guide to Early Printed Books and Manuscripts* – Wiley Blackwell, 2013

CRICK, JULIA and WALSHAM, A. – *The Uses of Script and Print, 1300-1700* – Cambridge University Press [CUP], 2004

DOYLE, A. I., RAINEY, E. and WILSON, D. B. – *Manuscript to Print* – Durham University, 1984

KILGOUR, FRED – *The Evolution of the Book* – Oxford University Press [OUP], 1998

LOVE, HAROLD – *The Culture and Commerce of Text: Scribal Publication in Seventeenth-Century England* – Massachusetts University Press, 1993

McKITTERICK, DAVID – *Print, Manuscript and the Search for Order* – CUP, 2003

RASMUSSEN, B. H. – *The Transition from Manuscript to the Printed Book* – OUP, 1962

SMITH, MARGARET M. – *The Title-Page: its early development 1460-1510* – British Library, 2000 (in the Reading Room shelved at 094)

ॐ   ॐ   ॐ

CHAPTER ELEVEN

How Books Were Funded

How was the printing of books financed?

WE HAVE SEEN that the production of manuscript books was relatively simple in financial terms: either the person wanting to purchase a copy contracted a scribe to produce one or he went to a stationer who would commission it for him and charge accordingly. Printing had expensive upfront costs with the related problem of having to produce a number of copies with no guaranteed customers that would defray the expenses quickly if the copies did not sell well.

Early printers would often find financial backers, eg: Gutenberg had the wealthy moneylender, Johann Fust; and they would try to print books with guaranteed sales. However, trying to guarantee sales often meant printing only the tried and tested, eg: Latin grammars and Bibles; and popular books already in circulation in manuscript, ie: Chaucer, religious texts, Roman and Greek classics. Most printed books until 1500 follow this model. The problem was overcoming risk when tackling living authors with new texts. Some printers would take the risk if they could balance it with a steady income from everyday printing jobs that had been commissioned and paid for, eg: indulgences, stationery, commercial circulars, proclamations, etc. But many printers failed financially.

How did new authors get published then?

Throughout the sixteenth century the normal way was for the author to approach an influential figure, normally someone aristocratic and wealthy, and offer to dedicate the book to them. The deal was that the patron might offer to fund the printing in exchange for a number of copies;

or to offer the author preferment, a place or a pension which would enable him to self-fund the printing; or simply to promote the book amongst his or her friends guaranteeing sales. The author would then put in the book an obsequious dedication to the patron and the patron would look to have his or her reputation enhanced by association with the writer's wit and erudition. Commercial sponsorship works in a similar way even today, eg: local firms sponsoring talks at the Wells Festival of Literature.

Edmund Spenser

In the Chained Library we have many examples of books printed by patronage. Edmund Spenser (1552-99) had dedicated his early work, *The Shepheardes Calender*, to Sir Philip Sidney who rewarded him with a post in the service of Lord Grey in Ireland. In Ireland he was able to write *The Faerie Queene* (our copy is the 1617 edition) at his leisure with further help from Sir Walter Raleigh when it came to printing. Sir Walter Raleigh (1554-1618) in turn received patronage for his *Historie of the World* from King James's eldest son, Prince Henry. An added advantage of having an influential patron was that it afforded a degree of protection and so made criticism of your work less likely.

When did the patronage system end?

The outright patronage with flattering dedications began to reduce as the court system itself weakened shortly before the Civil War, so by about the 1630s. However, it morphed into two other variants which were related.

Sir William Dugdale (1605-1686) insisted that his Antiquarian books should be well illustrated and we have had on display in 2015 examples of the work of Wenceslaus Hollar whose etchings Dugdale preferred. Dugdale partly financed these expensive books by asking aristocratic patrons to sponsor an illustration in return for having their coat of arms recorded on the print. The *Monasticum Anglicanum* of 1655 had fifty-two dedicated plates for which subscribers were asked to pay £5 per plate. This almost certainly also encouraged the patrons to buy copies for themselves and their friends.

Another system was used by John Minsheu to finance his *Ductor in linguas*, a multilingual dictionary in eleven languages, of which we have a copy of the first edition of 1617. Many claim that this is the first book printed by subscription but this is not strictly true. Minsheu did not receive money upfront from the purchasers. Instead, he first obtained academic endorsement of the book and then canvassed potential buyers and offered to list their names as purchasers when he printed the book. The temptation for the buyer was to be publicly associated with a prestigious book and to be named alongside the great and the good on the list of subscribers.

Example of a sponsored plate from Robert Plot's *Natural History of Oxford-shire, 1677.*

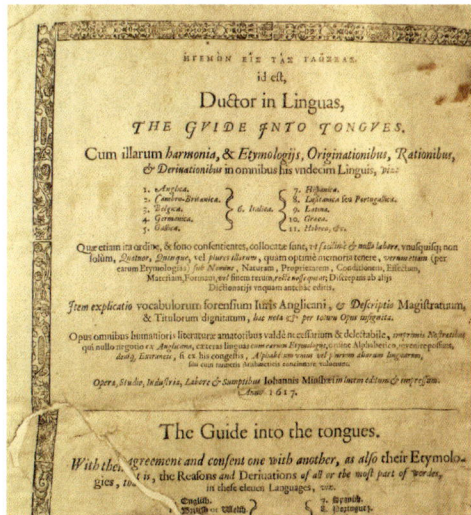

Minsheu's *Ductor in linguas*, 1617 (detail)

Did subscription publishing become common?

During the seventeenth century it was at first associated with large projects or with small circulation books such as poetry. A good example of seeking payment from buyers in advance of publication is Brian Walton's *Polyglot Bible* of 1657. This was a massive undertaking involving thirty-two scholars and four years of work to appear in six very large volumes. It prints out the earliest known texts of the Bible in Hebrew, Chaldaic, Samaritan, Syriac, Arabic, Persian, Ethiopian, Greek as well as the Vulgate Latin. To finance its publication, subscribers were sought who would pay £10 a set or £50 for six sets. Some 900 subscribers were found even though their names were not included in the book. We have two sets of this impressive work in the library, one belonging to Bath Abbey.

Many academic works were then financed in this way as the book buying population extended from the aristocracy to the gentry and the middle classes, and subscription publishing became a normal method of funding book production to the end of the eighteenth century.

Bishop Brian Walton's *Polyglot Bible* of 1657.

What were the problems of publishing by subscription?

Subscription publishing worked well enough and continues to this day, especially for books of local or specialist interest published by a recognised society or institution. However, the limitation in the seventeenth century and eighteenth century was that it relied on the author having a good network of friends and colleagues to find enough subscribers and picking a marketable product. One spectacular failure was the *Lexicon Heptaglotton* of Dr. Edmund Castell which was eventually published in 1669. Castell had worked on Walton's *Polyglot Bible* and intended his *Lexicon* as a comple-ment to it. Taking eighteen years and employing fourteen assistants to complete the work, he never managed to find sufficient subscribers and paid out £12,000 of his own money and ruined his health in the process. As many as 500 copies were remaindered and when he died these passed to his niece. She stored them in an unsound building and on her death the rat eaten remains sold for £7 in scrap paper.

How were the problems overcome?

Printers and booksellers were well aware of the shortcomings of the patronage and subscription models and many saw a commercial opportunity. From the earliest days of printing, many master printers like Caxton and Manutius had combined the role of printer and publisher. The publisher has to decide which books are going to sell, negotiate with the author, edit the content, and be responsible for the entire business of having the book produced, stored, marketed and delivered to a bookseller or to the buyer as well as bear the financial risk. The printer is only responsible for the physical production of the book. Over time these roles have often combined and we have seen printer/publishers, bookseller/publishers, bookseller/binders, etc. But in the eighteenth century the university presses and commercial firms like Longman (1724) began to develop their role such that publishing became a distinct occupation aided by the various copyright acts.

Today the traditional role of publisher has been threatened by new technology such that many authors can self-publish and deal directly with booksellers or market themselves via the internet and sell their work electronically. Similarly, academics can avoid the delays and selectivity of periodical publishers by distributing their work electronically.

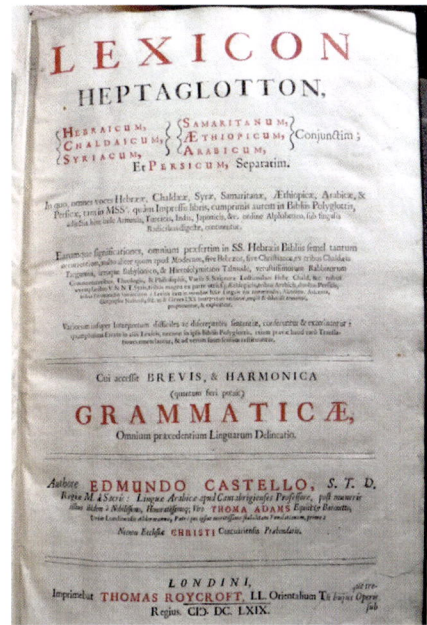

Edmund Castell's *Lexicon Heptaglotton* of 1669.

How else were books financed?

Within the period of the Chained Library, one can note the introduction of publishing by instalments. This allowed the publisher to gauge the market after the first few instalments and to quickly recoup costs to finance completion. It was mainly used for novels such as Samuel Richardson's *Clarissa* in the 1740s and then by Dickens in the nineteenth century, and also by some scientific publications.

WHERE CAN I READ MORE ABOUT THIS?

CLAPP, SARAH – *The Beginnings of Subscription Publishing in the Seventeenth century* – Modern Philology, Vol.29, Pt.2, Nov. 1931, pp.199-224

PARRY, GRAHAM – *Patronage and the Printing of Learned Works for the Author* – Cambridge History of the Book, Vol.4, 1557-1695 Chapter 7.

CHAPTER TWELVE

Seventeenth Century Literacy and Reading

Could all the cathedral clergy read and write in earlier times?

THE CANONS of the cathedral were always an educational elite. In Medieval times many of the bishops and deans occupied senior posts in government and were diplomats. Three examples from Wells in the 1400s were Nicholas Bubwith, our library's founder in 1424, who had been Lord High Treasurer of England; Thomas Beckington had been Lord Privy Seal and was sent on an embassy to Calais; John Gunthorpe had also been Keeper of the Privy Seal and was sent to Spain on a diplomatic mission. These men were valued as diplomats for their fluency in Latin in a Catholic Europe and their ability to relate to others in government positions still heavily influenced by a common religious culture. Both the Reformation in the 1500s and the ending of the court system in the early 1600s brought the dual role of cathedral clergy in both religious life and government service to an end. The last senior cleric to hold a government position is believed to be John Robinson, the Bishop of Bristol, who was made Lord Privy Seal in 1711.

During the sixteenth century and seventeenth century, when the Chained Library collection was built up, all but a handful of the cathedral clergy held degrees from Oxford or Cambridge (which were the only two English universities until the 1830s when Durham was founded). Only 5% had no degree at all, although they may have attended university but not graduated for various reasons. The majority held higher degrees. They had mainly been to grammar schools, which all taught Latin and grammar, with the majority having attended Westminster, Eton, Merchant Taylors' or Winchester schools; or they had been educated by private tutors.

What about the rest of the population?

It is wrong to think that illiteracy was widespread in the seventeenth century. Certainly women and the poor were likely to have been illiterate, but most villages had 'petty' schools that taught boys to read and write. It is thought that a third of males were literate by 1600. Literacy levels were largely linked to need, with professions such as lawyers and doctors being 100% literate, grocers 95%, but shepherds and labourers coming in at less than 10%. Despite Protestantism having given a huge boost to education with the encouragement to read the Bible, the church seemed to accept that the poor could get by as long as they could recite the catechism and listen to a sermon.

Literacy school

There was a large expansion of the grammar schools with charitable funding which might earlier have gone to the church before the Reformation. Between 1603 and 1649 some 142 new grammar schools, which all taught Latin and prepared boys for university, were established. University admissions rose from 800 a year in 1560 to over 1,200 in the 1630s, which gave a proportion of the eligible seventeen to eighteen year old population at university (2.3% of males) that was not exceeded in England until just after World War II.

What sort of books were people reading?

By 1600, printing was a fairly mature industry, and the range of material was not vastly different from that of today except that newspapers and periodicals did not exist. Today's readers of the tabloid press would have had pamphlets and chapbooks (short, inexpensive booklets often illustrated with woodcuts) telling them of murders, sudden deaths, strange happenings, monsters, witches, battles and happenings abroad, betrothals and marriages of the great, and deaths of kings and popes. These were sold at fairs and markets and those unable to read them could appreciate the pictures and usually know someone able to read to them. Reading at this time was not often silent and solitary but more likely to be collective and read out loud, especially given the low literacy rates of women.

The more educated could read political and religious pamphlets, plays, poems, books of self improvement and instructional manuals right up to the heavy duty academic books that characterise the Chained Library collection.

Reading out loud

Why were there no newspapers or magazines?

Single sheet or short newsbooks or corantos began circulating in the 1620s to give people information about events in Europe such as the Thirty Years' War. These were often manuscripts copied by scribes, and gentlemen would subscribe to receive them. During the Civil War in England, both sides printed news bulletins such as the Royalists' *Mercurius Aulicus*. A rudimentary postal service began in 1635 which aided circulation of these bulletins and the coffee houses became centres for the dissemination of their content from the 1650s.

The main reasons newspapers as we know them did not take off in the seventeenth century was censorship. The Licensing Acts of 1643 and 1662 were to control freedom of the press which the government saw as license to treason, and with a Civil War and Popish plots very much in mind it is easy to understand why such measures were introduced. We do not have a copy, but John Milton's *Areopagitica* of 1644 is still regarded as an eloquent plea for freedom of the press. The government also put a stamp duty on paper to discourage circulation of potentially seditious material. Besides, early newspapers were unattractive with bald facts without explanation or illustration and were mainly available only with a subscription. Many people would have thought that an ephemeral and expensive news sheet to be disposed of after a week or two was an extravagance they could not afford. And newspapers are very capital intensive to set up when neither government backing nor advertising are available. *The London Gazette* was established in 1666 but this was a government controlled organ which in its early days could be likened to *Pravda* .

It took the repeal of the Licensing Acts in 1695 to see publications similar to modern newspapers become a viable proposition. By 1704 there were four newspapers being printed in London and by 1709 there were nineteen. The term 'public opinion' was not used in English until 1781.

Periodicals began with the *Philosophical Transactions*, printed for The Royal Society, and we have in the Chained Library the first edition dated 6th March 1665. A few months before that, the *Journal des Sçavans* appeared in Paris and we also have some of the early copies of that more literary journal. Better known magazines like *The Tatler* commenced in 1709 and *The Spectator* in 1711.

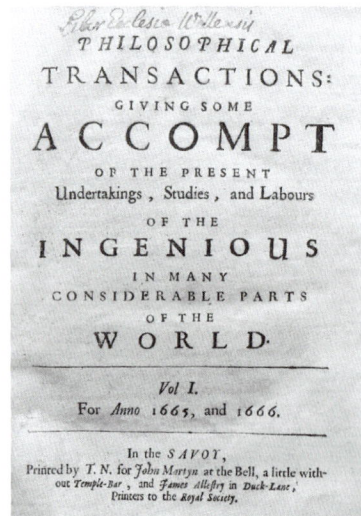

Title page of *Philosophical Transactions*

Were there any libraries to help people access books?

There were quite extensive private libraries belonging to the great and the good which they would probably have allowed their friends to use. But institutional libraries were confined to Oxford, Cambridge and the cathedrals given that monastic libraries had been destroyed at the time of the Reformation. Public libraries did not exist as we know them although a few charitable individuals had opened libraries in their home towns for the use of citizens, eg: the Francis Trigge library in Grantham (1598) and Humphrey Chetham's library in Manchester (1653), both of which still exist. Bristol also had a public library founded in 1613 which benefited greatly from a donation of books by Archbishop Mathew of York who was a native of the city. He gave his books "for the use of the Aldermen and Shopkeepers".

Parish churches would all have had a copy of the Bible for the public to read or be read to, and usually a copy of Foxe's *Book of Martyrs* and a copy of one of Erasmus' books. Only a few years ago the Rector of Saltford approached us saying he had an old book chained up in a glass case in the church which he thought might be valuable. It turned out to be a 1613 edition of the King James Bible. The binding was in poor condition, despite a Victorian rebinding, but the text block was in excellent condition. We agreed to rebind the book for him and he agreed to deposit it with us on loan as we did not have our own KJV. Our original copy was almost certainly lost during the Civil War when the cathedral library was moved to St. Cuthbert's church in Wells and no doubt certain prized books did not make the journey back on 14 May 1661.

Library provision improved in the eighteenth century. Towards the end of the seventeenth century the coffee houses were providing pamphlets for their clients and in the eighteenth century many had libraries of books. Learned societies such as The Royal Society, which was founded in 1660, would also have been developing libraries. Gentleman's clubs in the major cities formed in the eighteenth century and had libraries whilst at the same time some booksellers developed circulating libraries as a way of using surplus stock and to develop a new income stream . But public libraries as we know them had to wait until the 1850s.

How big were the private libraries?

It is thought that at least one third of households in England contained a single printed almanac by 1660. An almanac would have given simple reference material and prognostications. *Old Moore's Almanack*, which started in 1697, is still printed annually even today. Bibles would have been too expensive for many households but it is the book most likely to have been owned if people could afford one.

By 1700 it was not uncommon to find personal libraries of several hundred,

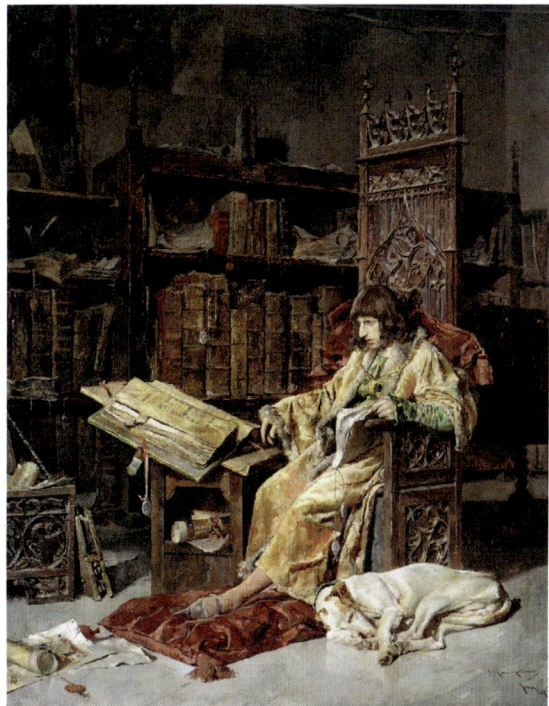

Prince Carlos of Viana in his library.

or even several thousand, books owned by scholars, clergymen, and gentry families, while tradesmen and the less well off might have a shelf's worth of devotional and popular works alongside a Bible. Large private libraries were unknown before the 1300s until Richard de Bury (1285-1345) amassed a collection of some 1,500 books and wrote the *Philobiblon,* one of the earliest books on librarianship. He was briefly the Dean of Wells in 1333 before becoming Bishop of Durham.

In the sixteenth century, most large, private libraries belonged to the higher echelons of the clergy, but there were exceptions like the library of Sir Thomas More (1478-1535), and the scholar, courtier and magician John Dee (1527-1609) who had collected between 3-4,000 books and manuscripts.

What sort of books were in these libraries?

The collection in the Chained Library is a very good reflection of a seventeenth century private library. There would typically be a sizeable proportion of theology (including works by the fathers of the church, biblical commentaries, devotional works, and contemporary controversy); a good number of books by Classical writers, along with varying amounts of history, poetry, geography and travel, science and natural history, mathematics, medicine, and law. Collections of any size, whether they belonged to clergymen, physicians, or noblemen usually contained such a broad range of recorded knowledge and had a high proportion of theological writings. Books would have been in Latin or English.

What happened to the libraries?

A few were sold at auction by the beneficiaries of wills, but the vast majority were given to colleges at Oxford and Cambridge or to the cathedral libraries. Almost all the cathedral libraries are dominated by the bequests of bishops. Here at Wells we benefit from the large bequests of Bishops Thomas Ken (1637-1711) and George Hooper (1640-1727). The library shelving had to be extended by three double-sided presses in 1728 to accommodate these bequests.

WHERE CAN I READ MORE ABOUT THIS?

BRIGGS, ASA and BURKE, PETER – *A Social History of the Media* – Polity, 2002

BURKE, PETER – *A Social History of Knowledge* – Polity, 2000

BURY, RICHARD DE – *Philobiblon* – (2 copies in the Reading Room at 010)

COWARD, BARRY – *The Stuart Age* – Longman, 2012

CRESSY, DAVID – *Levels of Illiteracy in England, 1530-1730* –
The Historical Journal, Vol.20, March 1977, pp.1-23

FOX, ADAM – *Oral and Literate Culture in England 1500-1700* – OUP, 2000

IRWIN, RAYMOND – *The English Library* – Allen & Unwin, 1966

LEHMBERG, STANFORD – *Cathedrals under Siege* – University of Exeter Press,
1996 (in the Reading Room at 270)

PEARSON, DAVID – *Patterns of Book Ownership in Late Seventeenth-Century
England* – Library, 2010, 11 (2), 139-67

STONE, LAURENCE – *The Educational Revolution in England, 1560-1640* –
Past and Present, XXVIII, 1964, pp.41-80

❧   ❧   ❧

CHAPTER THIRTEEN

The Seventeenth Century Book Trade

How many of the books are in Latin?

THERE ARE NO precise figures, but roughly half the books are in Latin. Use of Latin declined in the seventeenth century as a result of the Reformation, increased literacy and the preference of many writers to use the vernacular. Books printed in England were mainly in English simply because they could compete better in a niche market against the continental printers who had huge advantages of scale printing in Latin and with readier access to paper. The canons of the cathedral, who gave the books to the library, would all have been very competent in Latin from school and university where lessons and lectures were taught in Latin. Certain professions like medicine continued to use Latin and so did many early scientists as they saw this as a way to communicate across Europe to the educated elite. When Sir Isaac Newton published the first edition of *Philosophiae Naturalis Principia Mathematica* in 1687, the book was only available in Latin. However, in 1704, Newton's *Opticks* was published in English. (NB: Although we have many early science books, we have neither of these books by Newton). The year 1700 is thus a convenient break point for noting the decline in the use of Latin. The change from Latin to English can also be seen by comparing the origins of books in the chained library from the sixteenth century and seventeenth century.

In the sixteenth century, 90% of our books were printed in European cities such as Paris, Geneva, Antwerp, Venice, Frankfurt and Basle. But by the seventeenth century this had dropped to 31% as the English publishing industry was at last becoming competitive, although it was never regarded as the best source for learned and academic titles.

The imported books were mainly in Latin but with some ancient Greek and modern languages as well.

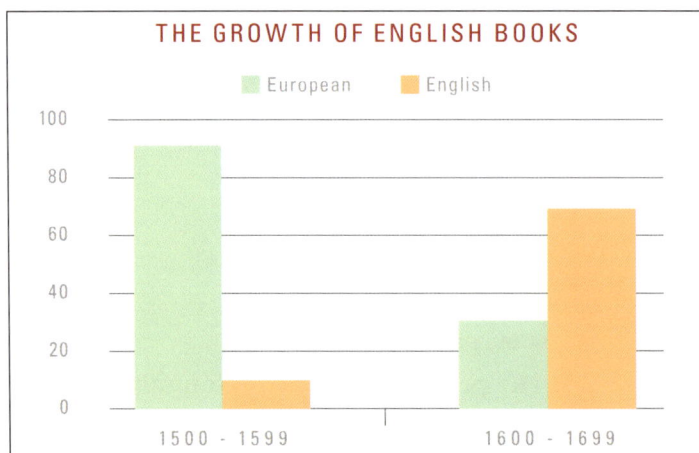

THE GROWTH OF ENGLISH BOOKS

European   English

1500 - 1599	1600 - 1699

Where could you buy books?

Bookshops were well established by the seventeenth century although called stationers in those days. The name stationer derives from the early practice of manuscript makers setting up their shop or station at a fixed location in the churchyard of St. Paul's cathedral in London, which differentiated them from itinerant sellers at fairs and markets. The scribes formed a Guild in 1403 which became the Stationers' Company in 1557 with headquarters next to St. Paul's where it continues today.

One imagines early bookshops in St. Paul's churchyard would have been similar to this contemporary example in Calcutta.

The book trade was heavily concentrated in London, which was only to be expected, given London's predominance. Only four towns in England had pop- ulations exceeding 10,000 (roughly the current popul- ation of Wells) by 1680: Norwich, Bristol, Newcastle and Exeter, whilst London had over 400,000. It was

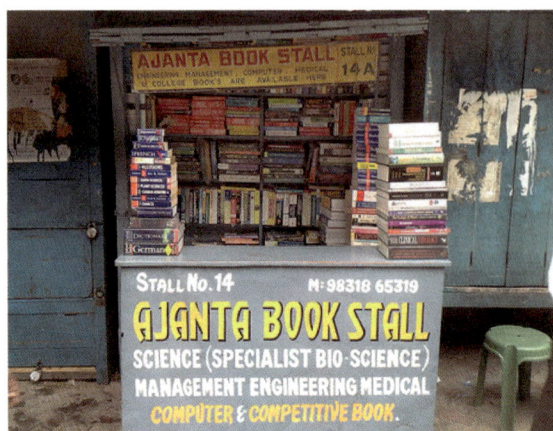

Calcutta book stall

also because most books were printed in London so that the authorities could monitor their production, and book imports from the continent were often similarly restricted to the London ports for ease of supervision. Most booksellers operated within the churchyard of St. Paul's cathedral or its immediate environs. Many of our books have on the title page directions to the publisher "at the sign of" in St. Paul's churchyard. Booksellers would lease their lock-up shops and often moved, so that it was important that they had a recognisable symbol for prospective customers to use in order to find them when they moved.

Directions to a bookshop in St. Paul's churchyard.

The Great Fire of London in 1666 destroyed most of the original shops and some £150,000 worth of books being stored in the crypt of St. Paul's. The booksellers re-established in the same location and there were reckoned to be 188 bookselling outlets in London by 1700. By that date bookshops were beginning to occupy their own premises.

Most provincial towns would have had a dedicated stationer by 1700, or at least a grocer or haberdasher who also retailed books. Many of the owners would have served their seven year apprenticeship with the Stationers Company in London and maintained their connections to the all important London centre. Provincial booksellers had good links to London by road or even sea and books requested by a reader would normally be transported in days. Provincial booksellers would also take their wares to seasonal fairs in their locality. The Stourbridge Fair near Cambridge was nationally famous and had an area dedicated to books. Isaac Newton is known to have bought a copy of Euclid's *Elements* at this Fair in 1665. Although selling second-hand books, the Provincial

Booksellers Fairs Association continues today to have a very active calendar of one day fairs in rented halls throughout the country.

Was there a book shop in Wells?

Cathedral cities usually attracted booksellers as the clergy would have been steady customers. There are no records covering the seventeenth century, but we know of one bookshop in Wells in the early part of the eighteenth century, run by a Mr Brown, and in the latter eighteenth century bookshops belonging to George (and/or John) Cass and John Evill, whose shop was in Sadler Street. Bath would have been a more obvious source for the canons but again Bath's main growth is associated with the eighteenth century.

The chained library is a collection of books given by the canons of the cathedral and it must be assumed that most of the bequests would have come at or near the end of their lives. The books would have been acquired over a lifetime and not just during their working life in Wells. If we take Bishop George Hooper (1640-1727), one of our great benefactors as an example, he gave some 244 books to the library at his death in 1727.

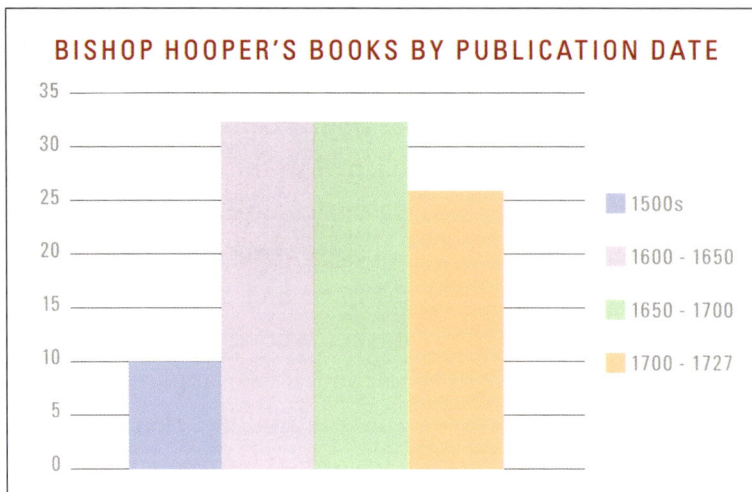

BISHOP HOOPER'S BOOKS BY PUBLICATION DATE

Legend: 1500s, 1600 - 1650, 1650 - 1700, 1700 - 1727

Checking the dates of publication of these books, only 26% of his books were published in the time of his bishopric. Some 42% were published before he was ten years old, although they could have been acquired during his time at Wells for all we know. But given his life of scholarship, that seems highly unlikely. Hooper may have acquired books from gifts or inheritance, but the likelihood is that almost half of his library was purchased second-hand.

So there was a good second-hand book market?

Very definitely. Books were solidly made of good paper and well bound so that they physically lasted well as we can see from our own library. Print runs tended to be quite short, perhaps 1,000 or 1,500 copies, so that books frequently went out of print and could only be acquired second-hand. Many booksellers would sell both new and second-hand books as, indeed, the Bailey Hill bookshop in Castle Cary still does today. Second-hand booksellers congregated in certain areas of London, especially at Moorfields, and Oxford and Cambridge would also have had a thriving trade in academic books being passed on to new generations of students and dons. An excellent example in our own collection is the 1472 Pliny *Historia Naturalis* that originally belonged to Dean John Gunthorpe and was lost from Wells at the time of the Reformation. On the flyleaf is a note saying that a later Dean, Dr. Ralph Bathurst, saw it for sale in a second-hand bookshop in Oxford in 1682, and seeing the provenance back to Gunthorpe, he purchased it and then later returned it to the chained library.

An early book auction

As well as bookshops, auctions of people's libraries were another source of second-hand books. Auction catalogues are known in Europe from as early as 1599 in Leiden, but the first catalogue from England is from an auction in London on 31st October 1675. Book auctions were often held in coffee houses and some 400 catalogues issued between 1675 and 1700 survive.

How did people know what books were available?

The number of titles available in the seventeenth century was only a fraction of what we can buy today. Booksellers would have used the Frankfurt Book Fair catalogue as a guide to what had been printed in Europe. Some individuals also procured copies of this Fair catalogue with John Dee being recorded as the first although York Minster library has a set from 1596-1623 which belonged to Archbishop Tobie Matthew. The Frankfurt Book Fair was certainly important by 1480 as a place where book publishers, printers, booksellers, binders, etc. could come together and learn what was happening as well as settle their accounts for books bought on credit or barter. Henry VIII sent Sir Thomas Bodley to the Fair to buy books for Oxford University. Although the Fair lost its pre-eminence to Leipzig for political and religious reasons for some 200 years, the revived Frankfurt Book Fair of today is still the most important date in the calendar every October for many in the book trade across the globe. Its catalogue was a respected and valued bibliographical tool even though it gave only bare details of author, title and publisher with no descriptive notes. An English edition began in 1617.

Printers in England would distribute copies of title pages as marketing tools to inform booksellers and customers of new publications. The Bodleian Library published its first printed catalogue in 1605, but obviously many of these books would not have been in print and readily available. It could alert scholars to what had been published so that searches for second-hand copies could be made. Publishers began listing their publications in the back of new books to advertise their wares from about the 1640s.

But the canons would largely have relied on booksellers who specialised in their interests to inform them of suitable publications available, whether new or second-hand, as well as correspondence from like-minded professionals or university contacts.

What was the difference in buying a book then and today?

Good booksellers in the seventeenth century would have known and trusted their customers well enough to package a number of new books for their perusal on a sale or return basis, more especially in the provinces. The practice of potential readers being invited to subscribe to have a book published was increasingly common. (The practice has not died out with local Somerset publisher Halsgrove recently funding many of its local publications in advance in the same way).

Perhaps the most obvious difference is that many books would arrive at the bookseller unbound. It was cheaper to transport books as blocks of text without binding material, and also many customers preferred to choose between cheap parchment covers and a variety of alternatives up to expensive panelled calf with gold tooling perhaps incorporating the family crest. Another common practice was for customers to have several small books bound into one book to save money. The technical term for such a multiple book is a sammelband. Our annotated book from the library of Thomas Cranmer dated 1512 is a good example as it incorporates three books. At that time Cranmer was a student at Cambridge and might have looked to keep his expenses down. Many booksellers were also bookbinders or certainly worked closely with them.

Why were there no book reviews?

The next chapter will look at the development of book reviewing, a practice we take for granted but which only developed in the later seventeenth century.

WHERE CAN I READ MORE ABOUT THIS?

CAMBERS, ADRIAN – *Godly Reading* – Cambridge University Press, 2011

JOHNS, ADRIAN – *The Nature of the Book* – University of Chicago Press, 1998

LEVY, F. J. – *How Information Spread Among the Gentry, 1550-1640* – J. of British Studies, Vol.21, No.2 Spring 1982, pp.11-34

RAVEN, JAMES – *The Business of Books* – Yale University Press, 2007

SHARPE, KEVIN – *Reading Revolutions* – Yale University Press, 2000

YEO, MATTHEW – *The Acquisition of Books by Chetham's Library, 1655-1700* – Brill, 2011

CHAPTER FOURTEEN

History of Book Reviews

When did book reviews first appear?

BOOKS WERE BEING NOTED in the newsbooks that both sides produced during the English Civil War of the 1640s. The Royalist journals *Mercurius Aulicus* and *Mercurius Rusticus* would trade insults with the Puritan equivalents such as *The Kingdom's Weekly Intelligencer*, condemning books and pamphlets issued by the other camp. Booksellers were also placing basic advertisements noting the author and title of new publications in these early newspapers to the extent that book notices comprised a considerable proportion of their content. It was difficult in the seventeenth century to learn what books were available and so the first steps in book reviewing were merely spreading awareness.

The first book reviews appeared in *Le Journal des Sçavans,* a French learned journal which began publication in January 1665. This was followed in March 1665 by the *Philosophical Transactions of the Royal Society* which contained scientific articles and also reviews of new books. The library is fortunate to have the very first issue of the *Philosophical Transactions* and a number of subsequent volumes as well as four volumes of the *Journal des Sçavans* from the 1670s which are in the Bath Abbey collection.

Why did it take 200 years after printing was invented for book reviews to be established?

The reasons why newspapers and periodicals were slow to develop were noted in Chapter Twelve on Literacy and Reading. Book reviews needed a printed vehicle that was up to date and fairly regular in order to reach their intended audience. Dedicated book review journals took even longer to be established and were first seen in the 1680s. Many of these would appear sporadically and lasted for only two or three years before ceasing publication. Journals might start as weekly, slip to monthly, and then become quarterly.

The irregularity of publication was because editors of these new journals faced many problems. They had TO BUY COPIES of the books as review copies were unknown. They had to find people to write the review when there was NO PAYMENT made and reviewers even had to RETURN THE BOOKS. Reviewers were ANONYMOUS so that it was seen as a low status task to be asked to review a book. Chasing people for copy when the POSTAL SYSTEM was rudimentary meant wasting large amounts of time, and the REWARDS FROM SUBSCRIPTIONS were meagre when people were unused to a NEW FORM OF PUBLICATION with an uncertain future. Editors often wrote the majority of reviews themselves and simply became EXHAUSTED in trying to keep the journal afloat.

Does the library have any of the early dedicated book review journals?

Bishop Thomas Ken (1637-1711) gave the library an almost complete set of the *History of the Works of the Learned, Or, an Impartial Account of Books Lately Printed in All Parts of Europe. With a Particular Relation of the State of Learning in Each Country*. This journal was one of the more successful and ran from 1699-1711 on a fairly monthly basis. As the title suggests, it had a focus on informing readers of philosophical, religious, scientific, historical and geographical books published on the continent which would have been quite readily available in London. It was edited by Jean de la Croze, a French Huguenot who had published a similar journal in Holland after becoming an exile. Our set is from 1699-1709.

The stated purpose of the journal was to assist "those who are less conversant with Books" and to enable them "to maintain Conversation with the Learned upon any subject, at a small Expence of Money and Time". So as not to limit its audience, it also made clear that it was not "wholly useless to the Learned, who may hence have a brief View of the Progress of Arts and Sciences in all Parts of Europe, and be thereby timely informed of such Books as may be proper for their Libraries". And to reassure the subscriber of its quality control, "We think fit likewise to assure the Reader, That we shall be so far from giving an

Account of Books that are Trifling, or contrary to good Manners, that we shall not so much as mention their Titles".

How impartial were the reviews?

Book reviews at this time were not analytical. They were often a short digest of the contents of a book and sometimes just a reprint of the Preface. Very often the content was plagiarised from another review journal or a translation into English from the continental original. The books reviewed were all non-fiction and fairly scholarly. Reviews of creative literature had to wait until the mid eighteenth century.

Title page of the first volume of *The Works of the Learned.*

Reviews were generally favourable in these early journals. As editors were always short of copy they requested authors to send in reviews of their own books. A number of the journals were printed by booksellers who obviously also had a vested interest in making their books sound worth buying. One of the most unscrupulous and quarrelsome was John Dunton (1659-1733), a London bookseller who had participated in the Monmouth Rebellion and fled to Virginia before returning when it was deemed safe to do so. He founded the Athenian Society which purported to be a group of experts but was really a group of four friends and relatives. The purpose of the Society was to produce a question and answer journal called the *Athenian Gazette*, which was forced to become the *Athenian Mercury* when the *London Gazette* complained of the similarity of title. Readers could send in questions and the 'experts' would answer them, although often the questions were placed by the experts and the answers frequently contained a recommendation to read one of Dunton's books.

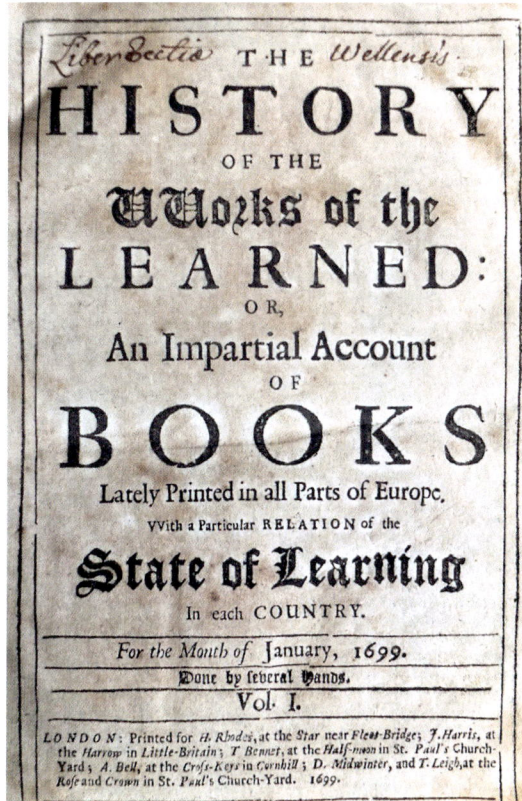

Dunton also produced a book review journal from 1692-4, *The Compleat Library or, News for the Ingenious*. This almost exclusively reviewed books from his bookshop.

ATHENIANISM *was John Dunton's thought.*
And in these features to Perfection brought;
For Knight and Gucht that Mystick Art did find
To paint John's PROJECTS *person and his Mind.*
They with the likeness, warmth and Grace do give
And make his Picture seem to think and live;

John Dunton

When did critical book reviewing begin?

The first successful literary magazine was the *Monthly Review*, founded in 1745 by Ralph Griffiths. It continued until 1845 and Griffiths edited it until his death in 1803. Part of the advertisement for the Review stated:

When the abuse of title-pages is obviously come to such a pass, that few readers care to take a book, any more than a servant, without a recommendation; to acquaint the public that a summary review of the productions of the press, as they occur to notice, was perhaps never more necessary than now, would be superfluous and vain.

The review would contain some fifteen full reviews but also added a brief catalogue note of other books deemed worthy of attention without a full review. By this time reviews covered the range of publishing output including fiction, poetry and plays. The lesser items only briefly catalogued were described elsewhere:

Such, however, as have cost less pains, are on an inferior scale, more in the style of mediocrity, or betray a structure less lofty, ornamental and finished, and occupy none of the higher walks of genius and taste, must be ranked with the common-place of the Month, and be content, as in other Reviews, with such brief notice as the Catalogue admits.

This idea that reviews were in a mediating position between booksellers and readers was fairly novel, and it brought criticism into the commercial centre of bookselling for the first time. The revolutionary change that reviewing brought in the relationship between authors, publishers and readers took place in the eighteenth century. Literary reputations could now be enhanced or reduced and even broken. By 1800 the *Monthly Review* had a circulation of 5,000, but it must be remembered that copies would have been available in coffee houses and so read by many more people.

What other review journals followed?

The first competitor was the *Critical Review* founded in 1756 with the novelist Tobias Smollett (1721-71) as its first editor.

In his inimitable style, Smollett laid out the prospectus for the new journal at the expense of its predecessor:

Tobias Smollett

This work [will be] ...executed by a Set of Gentlemen whose Characters and Capacities have been universally approved and acknowledged by the Public: Gentlemen who have long observed with Indignation the Productions of Genius and Dullness; Wit and Impertinence; Learning and Ignorance, confounded in the Chaos of Publication; applauded without Taste, and condemned without Distinction; and who have seen the noble Art of Criticism reduced to a contemptible Manufacture subservient to the most sordid Views of Avarice and Interest, and carried on by wretched Hirelings, without Talent, Candour, Spirit or Circumspection.

Despite the bombast, it was very similar to the *Monthly Review* and attracted contributions from Samuel Johnson, David Hume and Oliver Goldsmith.

Shortly after, the *London Review* began in 1775, the *English Review* in 1783, the *Analytical Review* in 1788, the *Edinburgh Review* in 1802, the *Quarterly Review* in 1809, *Blackwood's Edinburgh Magazine* in 1817 and the *Westminster Review* in 1824. Many of these became quite independent of the booksellers and so the impartial reviews of today were born.

WHERE CAN I READ MORE ABOUT THIS?

BARNES, SHERMAN – *The Editing of Early Learned Journals* – Osiris, Vol.1, Jan. 1936, pp.155-72

FORSTER, ANTONIA – *Book reviewing* – Chapter 33 in *Cambridge History of the Book 1695-1830* – Cambridge University Press, 2009

GAEL, PATRICIA – *The Origins of the Book Review in England, 1663-1749* – The Library, Vol.13, March 2012, pp.63-89

McCUTCHEON, PHILIP – *The Beginnings of Book-Reviewing in English Periodicals* – Proceedings of the Modern Language Association, Vol.37, Dec. 1922, pp.691-706

PARKS, STEPHEN – *John Dunton and the Works of the Learned* – The Library, Vol.23, 1968 pp.13-24

CHAPTER FIFTEEN

Contents of other Cathedral Libraries

Do we know anything about the historic use of the Chained Library's books ?

W E DO NOT HAVE any records as to who borrowed or read which books in the Chained Library. In fact, apart from a list of forty-six books made by John Leland when he visited in the 1530s, the Benefactors' Book of the seventeenth century, and a handwritten, but thorough, catalogue of the contents in 1734, we do not know a great deal about the history of the library as a working library.

However, in 1964, Professor Paul Kaufman, of the University of Washington in Seattle, wrote about his research in to the use of eight cathedral libraries in England during the eighteenth century. His research was detailed over four issues of the *Bulletin of the New York Public Library* and includes all of the raw data as to which books were borrowed and how many times. What it reveals is the remarkable similarity of the printed book contents of these eight libraries, and because we have the titles of all the books, we can see that Wells also had a very similar collection. And because the use of the books is again very similar, we can reasonably assume that the use patterns identified by Kaufman would also be applicable in Wells.

The eight cathedral libraries from which his data came all have ledgers recording loans during the years indicated

So were the libraries well used?

We must recognise that Kaufman's data only covers loans of books and so does not include reference use of the books in the library. But if we take the total number of years of loans recorded as 581, and the total

CATHEDRAL	YEARS	BORROWERS	LOANS
Canterbury	1797-1819	47	1,884
Carlisle	1703-1803	90	1,401
Durham	1711-1801	231	6,364
Exeter	1751-1799	43	1,323
Gloucester	1730-1800	97	1,118
St Paul's	1744-63, 1783-1821	57	726
Winchester	1728-1820	81	1,384
York	1716-1820	179	1,241
Totals	581 years	825	15,251

number of loans recorded as 15,251, we can see that an average of twenty-six books were borrowed each year from each library. This figure seems low, but then these libraries were the private libraries of the Dean and Chapter and so the number of people entitled to borrow books was also very low. And by the eighteenth century, many Canons would have been able to afford books of their own.

Kaufman records that 825 names were identified from the loan ledgers. Averaging out the total of loans by the number of borrowers would give a figure of just over eighteen loans per borrower. However, this average is fairly meaningless as he also records that a small number of users made disproportionate use of the library. In the case of Canterbury, one individual made 434 loans and seven others borrowed more than fifty books. Durham shows twenty-five individuals borrowing more than fifty books and two with totals over 500. Many loans would have been the same book borrowed by an individual more than once.

Who were the users?

85-90% of the loans were made to the Chapter or the cathedrals' canons. The other borrowers were a mix of clerical or laymen (only twenty women unrelated to members of the Chapter are recorded as having managed to borrow books). The laymen could be classed as 'the great and the good' being theologians, antiquarians, doctors, politicians and writers. Most of them have entries in the *Dictionary of National Biography*. Perhaps the best known is Samuel Taylor Coleridge who borrowed books from both Carlisle and Durham. The novelist Laurence Sterne borrowed from York Minster.

Did laymen borrow from Wells cathedral library?

I think we can reasonably assume that a few local clergymen and laymen would have had access to the library on a reference only basis if not for loans. There are only two people who can be identified. Dr. Claver Morris (1659-1727) was a well-known local physician and also a musician who played music in the Deanery. We have a printed copy of his diary in the Reading Room which notes that he was allowed to show some visitors around the library and he also gave a book to the library. The second is the Rev. John Skinner (1772-1839) who was the Rector of Camerton. In his diary entry of 13 August 1817 he records, "I afterwards went over to the Cathedral, escorted by Mr Sherston, and spent some time in the library. If I lived in the neighbourhood it would be a pretty constant attraction."

Which subjects were popular?

Unsurprisingly for the time, Divinity and Bible studies, Classical writers and History make up two thirds of all the loans. The proportions of loans in the table below is very much reflected in the numbers of books in the collection at Wells and it seems highly likely our loan pattern would be the same.

SUBJECT	%
Divinity and Ecclesiastical history and biography	29
Bible texts and commentaries	8
History and Antiquities	19
Greek and Latin	10
Travel and Geography	6
English and modern European literature	5
Mathematics and Science	4
Dictionaries — mainly language	4
Law and government	3
Philosophy	3
Arts and Music	3

Can we identify particular books that were well used?

Our strength is in printed books of the seventeenth century and some of the cathedrals analysed by Professor Kaufman have books published in the late eighteenth century that we do not have. But of the books we do have, the following are the most borrowed [*see overleaf*]:

DIVINITY

ST. AUGUSTINE – *Works*

BARROW, ISAAC – *Works*, 1686

BURN, RICHARD – *Ecclesiastical Law*, 1763

ST. JOHN CHRYSOSTOM – *Works*

DUGDALE, WILLIAM – *Monasticon Anglicanum*, 1661

ECTON, JOHN – *Thesaurus Rerum Ecclesiasticum*, 1763

GIBSON, EDMUND – *Codex Juris Ecclesiastici Anglici*, 1713

HOOKER, RICHARD – *Of the Lawes of Ecclesiastical Politie*, 1617

STILLINGFLEET, EDWARD – Various works

STRYPE, JOHN – *Ecclesiastical Memorials*, 1721

TANNER, THOMAS – *Notitia Monastica*, 1695

TILLOTSON, JOHN – Various works

BIBLE

NEW TESTAMENT IN GREEK – 1707

CALMET, AUGUSTINE – *Dictionary of the Bible* (3 vols.), 1732

HAMMOND, HENRY – *Paraphrase on the New Testament*, 1689

HORNE, GEORGE – *Commentary on the Psalms* (2 vols.), 1776

LOWTH, ROBERT – *Translation of Isiah*, 1778

NEWTON, THOMAS – *Dissertations on the Prophecies*, 1760

PATRICK, SIMON – *Commentary on the Historical Books of the Old Testament*, 1738

PRIDEAUX, HUMPHREY – *Old and New Testament Connected*, 1718

WALTON, BRIAN – *Polyglot Bible* (6 vols.), 1657

WHITBY, DANIEL – *Paraphrase and Commentary on the New Testament*
(2 vols.), 1706

HISTORY AND ANTIQUITIES

BURNET, GILBERT – *History of the Reformation of the Church of England*
(3 vols.), 1679

CAMDEN, WILLIAM – *Britannia*, 1695

DUGDALE, WILLIAM – *History of St. Paul's*, 1658

HUME, DAVID – *History of England* (6 vols.), 1762

JOSEPHUS, FLAVIUS – *Works*, 1720

ROBERTSON, WILLIAM – *History of America* (2 vols), 1778

ROBERTSON, WILLIAM – *History of Charles V* (4 vols.), 1772

GREEK AND LATIN

The works of Horace, Livy, Tacitus and Vergil were the most borrowed. And within **Dictionaries**, it is the Greek and Latin dictionaries that were most in demand.

TRAVEL

CAPTAIN JAMES COOK'S three voyages are far and away the most borrowed
WHELER, GEORGE – *A Journey into Greece*, 1682

MATHEMATICS AND SCIENCE

The Philosophical Transactions of the Royal Society are by far the most used. We have the very first copy of 1665 and subsequent until 1669 and then 1700-1730.

LAW AND GOVERNMENT

BLACKSTONE, WILLIAM – *Commentaries on the laws of England* (4 vols.), 1768
RYMER, THOMAS – *Foedora* (20 vols.), 1704-35

PHILOSOPHY

LOCKE, JOHN – *Works* (4 vols.), 1722

ARTS AND MUSIC

SPENCE, JOSEPH – *Polymetis*, 1749

WHERE CAN I READ MORE ABOUT THIS?

BOTFIELD, BERIAH – *Notes on Cathedral Libraries* – Pickering, 1849
  (in the Reading Room at 027)
HOBHOUSE, EDMUND – *The Diary of a West Country Physician* (Claver Morris)
  – Simpkin Marshall, 1934 (in the Reading Room shelved at 920MOR)
KAUFMAN, PAUL – *Reading Vogues at English Cathedral Libraries of the Eighteenth
  Century* – Bulletin of the New York Public Library, Vols.67 and 68, December
  1963; and Jan/Feb/March 1964 (in the Reading Room shelved at 026)
REYNOLDS, HERBERT – *Our cathedral Libraries: their history, contents and uses*
  – Chiswick Press, 1879 (in the Reading Room shelved at 026 oversize)
SKINNER, JOHN – *Journal of a Somerset Rector* Kingsmead Press, Bath, 1971
  (not the 1930 edition)

CHAPTER SIXTEEN

A Sequence of Bibles

What is the oldest Bible in the library?

W E HAVE A COMPLETE BIBLE in manuscript from the thirteenth century [*see below*]. The Bible is small at about A5 size and the writing is minute. The parchment is wafer thin and used the skins of unborn calves which were often split into two or three layers. It is likely to have been produced in Paris. These French portable Bibles are associated with the advent of Franciscan and Dominican friars. Until the thirteenth century, Bibles had been very large and normally would have needed several volumes to make a complete text. But by the thirteenth century there were commercial workshops producing manuscript books for the new university and they were able to make books in far greater numbers than the monasteries had done.

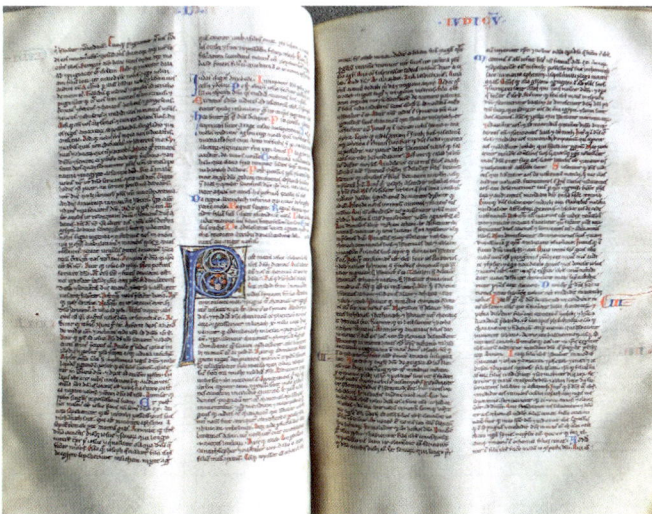

A complete portable Bible in manuscript, possibly from Paris. Thirteenth century.

The attraction of a small book was not just the portability. By having the complete text in one volume, there was a feeling that it was definitive, representing and enclosing the totality of the word of God. These Paris Bibles do not have the heavy illumination of the larger volumes but normally red and blue decoration with the occasional gold highlights. This Bible was not part of the original pre-Reformation collection. It was given to the library in 1863 by the Rev. Charles Sydenham, rector of Brushford.

What is the oldest printed Bible in the library?

In the Bath Abbey collection there is a Bible printed in Venice in 1498 by Simon Bevilaqua. This is a Latin Vulgate and qualifies as an incunabula as it was printed before 1501.

Do you have a Gutenberg Bible?

Sadly not. The Gutenberg Bible of 1455 was printed in Mainz by Johannes Gutenberg and is generally accepted as the first printed book. It is in Latin and follows the Vulgate version of the Catholic church. Some 175 copies were made of which twenty-one complete copies survive. Of the twenty-one copies, six are in England: at Eton College, The Bodleian in Oxford, Cambridge University Library, The John Rylands in Manchester; the British Library has two, and there is a New Testament only at Lambeth Palace. Interestingly, none of the surviving complete or imperfect copies held around the world are in a cathedral library.

The Gutenberg Bible is highly treasured because of its rarity and beauty, and if a copy came to auction today it would probably fetch upwards of £20 million. There is a facsimile copy of the Gutenberg Bible in the Reading Room at 220.4.

What is the earliest Bible in English in the library?

The Chained Library has a good number of Bibles in English but most of the more famous ones are not represented. The assumption is that when the library moved to St. Cuthbert's church in Wells during the Civil War, many of our Bibles would have gone missing at that stage. As an example, in 2011 when the country celebrated the 400th anniversary of the King James Bible, we did not have an early edition to put on display and yet the cathedral would certainly have had one on publication.

It may be helpful to run through the better known Bibles and indicate which ones we have and those that we do not have.

Wyclif Bible 1380-1395 (*We do not have*)

John Wyclif (c.1320-1384) was an eminent philosopher and theologian in holy orders who became Master of Balliol College, Oxford. He believed the Bible should be available in English and translated the Catholic Vulgate Bible with some help from other academics. The translation was very literal and quite difficult to follow and has not played any part in subsequent translations. Copies of the Wyclif Bible were all handwritten and appeared in the 1380s and 1390s. As the authorities thought it heretical to own a Bible in English, punishment was severe if anyone was found with a copy. Despite this, some 250 manuscript copies survive. Wyclif's persecuted followers were known as Lollards. His contribution has led to him being acclaimed the "Morning Star of the Reformation".

John Wyclif

Tyndale Bible 1526 (*We do not have*)

William Tyndale (1494-1536) was another believer that the Bible should be available in English. By his time, Erasmus had translated the New Testament from the original Greek into a new Latin version which the Protestant reformers felt was more accurate than the Catholic Vulgate of St. Jerome written in about AD 400. The library has a 1539 printing of the Erasmus translation. Tyndale was also encouraged by Martin Luther's translating the Bible into German.

His attempts to have an English translation authorised by the Church of England were rebuffed by Cuthbert Tunstall, the Bishop of London, and eventually Tyndale went into exile in Europe to complete his new translation. He was fluent in eight languages including Greek, Hebrew and Latin. The first printing of the New Testament was made at Worms in 1526 and copies were smuggled in to England by sea. Tunstall burned all the copies that could be discovered. Now, only two complete copies of this first printing of 3,000 exist, one at the British Library which was bought in 1994 for over £1 million from the Bristol Baptist College. An American institution would have paid more but was denied an export licence. The other was found in the last century in a German monastery and then transferred to the Wurttemberg State Library in Stuttgart. Tyndale never completed his translation of the Old Testament, but his translation of the Pentateuch (Genesis, Exodus, Leviticus, Numbers, Deuteronomy) was published later in 1530. So no complete Bible in English was ever issued in Tyndale's name.

Tyndale was persecuted for his heresy, especially by Sir Thomas More, who was Lord Chancellor, and his imprisonment and execution by being burnt at the stake in Antwerp in 1536 was the result of More's vindictiveness towards Tyndale. (By 1534 the Canterbury Convocation had agreed that a translation into English should be made.) Tyndale's work lives on in that the *King James Bible* of 1611 is estimated to use 84% of Tyndale's New Testament and 76% of his Old Testament translation, much of it word for word.

Coverdale Bible 1535 (*We do not have*)

Miles Coverdale (1488-1569) was much more of an establishment figure than Tyndale. He was originally an Augustinian friar, like Martin Luther, and lived in exile in Europe from 1528-1535 where he worked with Tyndale as his amanuensis. The Coverdale Bible printed in Antwerp in 1535 was the first complete Bible printed in English. It comprised Tyndale's New Testament and Pentateuch but the remainder of the Old Testament was Coverdale's translation based on Luther's German

Miles Coverdale

translation and the Vulgate texts. Unlike Tyndale, Coverdale had no fluency in Greek or Hebrew. His Bible was later reprinted in England in 1539 with a royal licence and so was the first officially approved translation of the Bible into English. Copies are not rare as it went through twenty editions until 1553. That Coverdale had developed good relations with Thomas Cromwell and Thomas More, as well as the patronage of Anne Boleyn, enabled him to escape Tyndale's fate.

Matthew Bible 1537 (*We do not have*)

Another exile who worked with Tyndale was John Rogers (1505-55). The Matthew Bible differs from the Coverdale Bible in using not only Tyndale's New Testament, but all of the translation of the Old Testament that Tyndale had translated from Hebrew before his death, ie: the Pentateuch and ten other books. The Old Testament is completed by Coverdale's translation from German and Latin. Rogers's main contribution is a translation of the Prayer of Manasses in the Apocrypha and the notes on the text, a calendar, almanac and the general editing. He used the pseudonym Thomas Matthew as he could not acknowledge the 'heretic' Tyndale, and so he used the names of two disciples. The book was printed at first in Hamburg, but later in London under royal licence.

Despite Rogers' caution with the pseudonym, he was burnt at the stake by Queen Mary in 1555, becoming the first Protestant martyr of her reign. His courageous death was witnessed by his wife and eleven children.

Taverner's Bible 1539 (*In the library*)

Richard Taverner (1505-75), was encouraged by Thomas Cromwell to make this translation. It is essentially a revision of the Matthew Bible using Taverner's strong Greek scholarship and less strong Hebrew skills. It is not regarded as particularly significant. Our copy dates from 1551 and was given to the library by Bishop Robert Creighton (1670-2).

Great Bible 1539, sometimes called the Cromwell Bible (*1541 edition in the library*)

Our copy of the Great Bible dates from 1541 and is also known as CRANMER'S BIBLE as he added a preface to the earlier 1539 edition. However, our copy was in the Vicars Choral library and is in poor condition generally and has no preface.

It is called Great simply because of its size. Cromwell ordered that every church should have a copy of this Bible in the largest format possible so that parishioners could see it. It thus became the first Authorised Version. It was edited by Miles Coverdale and is taken from the translation of Tyndale, his own, but also the Matthew Bible. Some 2,500 copies were printed, at first in Paris and then in London. The authorities eventually took fright at the freedom of the people to read the Bible in English and by 1546 there was a prohibition of all Bibles in English except the Great Bible which was so large few people could afford to buy one. When Edward VI came to the throne in 1547, the prohibition was reversed and all were reprinted.

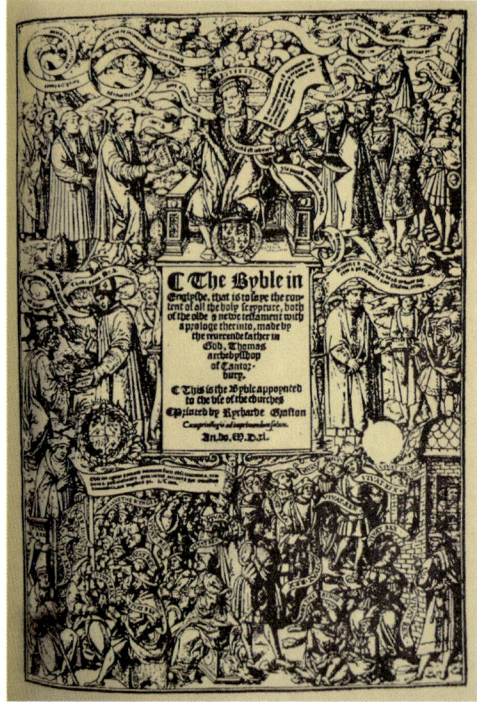

Great Bible showing Henry VIII giving copies to Thomas Cranmer and Thomas Cromwell

Geneva Bible 1560 (*In the library*)

During Queen Mary's reign, 1553-8, a number of Protestant scholars fled to Geneva to join notable Protestants such as John Calvin and Theodore Beza. They decided to produce a Bible which would have marginal explanatory notes, maps, tables, woodcut illustrations and indices. The basic translation was that of Tyndale but scholars also completed his work on the translation of the Old Testament from the original Hebrew.

The printer Robert Estienne in Paris added verse numbers. The Bible was made more attractive by being printed in smaller quarto and octavo sizes. This made it affordable, and the Roman type made it more readable than the usual black letter or Gothic type. It became hugely popular, especially amongst Puritans and dissenters, and was the Bible taken to America by the Pilgrim Fathers. Oliver Cromwell's men preferred this version during the Civil War.

In 1579 a variation appeared with a translation of Genesis 3:7 that says "and they sewed figge leaves together, and made themselves breeches". This version became known as the BREECHES BIBLE which is a name sometimes given to any version of the Geneva Bible.

Bishops' Bible 1568 (*We do not have*)

In Queen Elizabeth I's reign, the Great Bible and the Geneva Bible were the two most frequently used Bibles. The Great Bible was deemed deficient in that much of the Old Testament was the translation by Coverdale using the Vulgate and not the original Hebrew. The Geneva Bible was not popular with the Church of England hierarchy because of its Puritan origins which encouraged the abolition of bishops and a church led by lay elders.

Mathew Parker, as Archbishop of Canterbury, commissioned a committee of bishops to revise the earlier translations. The mistake was not to appoint a supervising editor so that there are many inconsistencies, and the Bible was printed in a large format as it was intended to be used in the pulpit rather than to be owned privately. It was beautifully illustrated and finely printed, but it was never popular, lacking the simplicity and quality of the Geneva translation as well as its more convenient size. It amounted to a minor revision of the Great Bible.

Because it reads in Jeremiah 8:22 "Is there not treacle at Gilead?", the word treacle changing to balm in the KJV of 1611, the Bishops' Bible is also known as the TREACLE BIBLE.

Although we do not have a copy of this Bible, we have William Fulke's 1617 New Testament showing in parallel text the Rheims and the Bishops' Bible versions.

Douai-Rheims Bible 1582 New Testament and 1609/10 Old Testament (*In the library*)

The Roman Catholic Church decided that one response to the Protestant Reformation was to make their own translation of the Bible into English. The work was done by scholars in Douai (OT) and Rheims (NT) and they translated from the Latin Vulgate. The marginal notes were intended to reinforce the Catholic interpretation of the Bible and to uphold Catholic tradition. The translation is ecclesiastical and Latinate rather than colloquial, but a number of the terms introduced found their way into the King James Bible.

King James Bible 1611 (*1613 edition in the library*)

King James I had been brought up in Scotland and had shown no great love for the Presbyterians north of the border. When he became King of England in 1603, Puritans made it known that they were not content with either of the authorised versions, ie: the Great Bible and the Bishops' Bible. King James in turn was not enamoured of the popular Geneva Bible owing to its Calvinistic tone and lack of deference to the monarchy's powers. At a conference in 1604, King James commissioned a new translation from the original Greek, Hebrew and Aramaic. The work would be carried out by six committees of forty-seven Church of England divines. The committees took four years and the editing then led to a first printing of the third Authorised Version in 1611. (Owing to a typographical error in some printings of Ruth 3:15, some versions are referred to as "HE BIBLES" instead of the correct "SHE BIBLES"). Their instructions had been to avoid notes and illustrations and to make the text support the episcopal structure of the Church of England including ordained ministers.

Another of the famous Bible errata was the WICKED BIBLE of 1631. Robert Barker was the royal printer and in a reprint his compositors missed out "not" so that the instruction read "Thou shalt commit adultery". He was fined £300 by the Star Chamber, having offended Charles I, and also lost his licence to print Bibles.

Our original copy of the KJV went missing, probably during the Civil War. But in 2012 the Rector of Saltford church, between Bath and Bristol, brought in a 1613 copy that been chained up at the back of his church. The binding was in poor condition but the text block was in surprisingly good condition. An agreement was reached whereby we rebound the book at our expense for which we will be allowed to keep it in the Chained Library on loan from Saltford.

King James I of England (also James VI of Scotland).

What is a Polyglot Bible?

Polyglot Bibles show the same text of the Bible in several different languages to assist scholars in their interpretation from different sources. The earliest attempt at such a book was the *Hexapla* of Origen in about AD 240, which showed six versions but only in Greek and Hebrew. There is a copy of this in the Chained Library printed in Paris in 1713.

The first real Polyglot was the COMPLUTENSIAN commissioned by Cardinal Jiménez de Cisneros. This was printed in six volumes between 1514/7 at Alcalà de Henares near Madrid. It shows Hebrew, Latin, Chaldean and Greek and was published in 1522, the publication being delayed because Erasmus had been granted a four year privilege on his own 1517 translation of the New Testament from the original Greek.

The next was the ANTWERP POLYGLOT sponsored by Philip II of Spain and edited by Arias Montanus. It was printed in Antwerp by Christopher Plantin between 1569-72 and added a Syriac New Testament. We have a set of this Bible given by Bishop Arthur Lake (1616-26).

The PARIS POLYGLOT followed in 1645 adding the Syriac Old Testament and parts of the Bible in Samaritan and Arabic. We do not have a set.

The last of the great Polyglot Bibles was the LONDON POLYGLOT edited by Bishop Brian Walton and published in 1657. It is in six volumes and it added versions of the New Testament in Ethiopian and parts of the Old Testament in Persian to give nine possible languages. The work has not been superseded. Some 1,000 copies were made, 900 being purchased in advance at a subscription price of £10. The Chained Library has a copy purchased originally by an estate in East Harptree whose armorial binding it still carries, and given to the cathedral by Thomas Holt, Chancellor of Wells Cathedral from 1660-89. The Bath Abbey collection also has a set.

Do you have Bibles in foreign languages?

There are a number of Bibles in original languages such as Greek, Hebrew, Syriac and Chaldean. In addition, we have Bibles in Italian (1562), French (1588), Arabic (1616), Welsh (1620 and fragments of the earlier translation into Welsh of 1567), German (1622, the Martin Luther version printed in Wittenberg), Dutch (1657) and Spanish (1661).

Do you have copies of the holy books of other religions?

We have three copies of the *Koran*, something that surprises many visitors. There is a copy in Arabic that belonged to Bishop George Hooper (1703-27), a distinguished orientalist, which dates from 1694. And we have the two earliest translations into English. The 1649 translation by Alexander Ross was made from a French translation and is not highly regarded. The 1734 translation directly from Arabic was made by George Sale and is more scholarly.

The Chained Library also has a number of Jewish texts. There are five copies of the *Biblia Hebraica,* the earliest of which dates from 1543. There are several versions of the *Mischnah*, the collection of oral laws and traditions compiled in about AD 200 that forms part of the Talmud. And an extensive collection of the works of Maimonides, the influential rabbi born in Cordoba who lived at the end of the twelfth century, which includes his *Mischneh Torah* detailing Jewish observance in fourteen books.

৵

WHERE CAN I READ MORE ABOUT THIS?

BOBRICK, BENSON – *The Making of the English Bible* – Weidenfeld, 2001

BRAGG, MELVYN – *The Book of Books: the radical impact of the King James Bible 1611-2011* – Hodder 2011

BRAKE, DONALD L. – *A Visual History of the English Bible* – Baker, 2008 (in the Reading Room at 220.9)

BRUCE, F. F. – *History of the Bible in English* – Lutterworth, 1979 (In the Reading Room at 220.9)

CAMPBELL, GORDON – *Bible: the story of the King James Version* – OUP, 2010 (In the Reading Room at 220.9)

CRYSTAL, DAVID – *Begat: the King James Bible and the English language* – OUP, 2010 (In the Reading Room at 220.52)

DANIELL, DAVID – *The Bible in English: its history and influence* – Yale UP, 2003 (In the Reading Room at 220.9)

DANIELL, DAVID – *William Tyndale: a biography* – Yale UP, 2001

DE HAMEL, CHRISTOPHER – *The Book: a history of the Bible* – Phaidon, 2001 (in the Reading Room at 220.9)

ENGLISH HEXAPLA – Exhibiting the six important translations of the New Testament scriptures (Wiclif 1380, Tyndale 1534, Great Bible 1539, Geneva 1557, Rheims 1582, King James 1611) – Bagster, 1841 (In the Reading Room at 220)

EVANS, G. R. – *John Wyclif* – Lion, 2005

McGRATH, ALISTER – *In the Beginning: the story of the King James Bible* – Hodder, 2001 (In the Reading Room at 220.5)

NICHOLSON, ADAM – *Power and Glory: Jacobean England and the making of the King James Bible* – Harper, 2003

PRICE, DAVID and RYRIE, CHARLES – *Let it go Among our People: an illustrated history of the English Bible from John Wyclif to the King James Version* – Lutterworth, 2004

WHITE, ERYN – *The Bible in Welsh* – History Press, 2007 (in the Reading Room at 220.542)

CHAPTER SEVENTEEN

The Book of Common Prayer

Do you have an early Book of Common Prayer?

WHEN the Church of England renounced papal authority with the Act of Supremacy in 1534, the pattern of Catholic church services had to be replaced. A priority was to produce a prayer book in English indicating the renunciation of Rome. The task fell to Thomas Cranmer, who was Archbishop of Canterbury from 1533 until his execution in 1556.

The first Book of Common Prayer [*hereafter referred to by the abbreviation* BCP] was published in 1549, in the reign of Edward VI. Prayer books, unlike books of prayers, contain the words of structured (or liturgical) services of worship. The work of 1549 was the first prayer book to contain the forms of service for daily and Sunday worship in English and to do so within a single volume; it included morning prayer, evening prayer, the Litany, and Holy Communion. The book included the other occasional services in full: the orders for baptism, confirmation, marriage, 'prayers to be said with the sick' and a funeral service.

The 1552 Book of Common Prayer

It set out in full the Epistle and Gospel readings for the Sunday Communion Service. Set Old Testament and New Testament readings for daily prayer were specified in tabular format as were the set Psalms; and canticles, mostly biblical, that were provided to be sung between the readings.

We do not have a 1549 BCP but we do have a 1552 BCP. The 1549 Book was always regarded as more of a first draft awaiting revision. The 1552 revision removed practices that could have been regarded as more Catholic. It had only a short life as, on the death of Edward VI in 1553, his Catholic half-sister Mary I restored union with Rome. On her death, a slightly revised version was published in 1559 and was not superseded until 1662. We do not have a copy of the 1559 BCP.

Do you have any of the earlier Catholic liturgies?

Before the Reformation, Roman Catholic worship varied slightly across the country. In most of southern England, the Sarum Rite, based on practice developed in Salisbury in the eleventh century, was followed and that included Wells.

As we lost our earlier library at the time of the Reformation, we have none of our original service books. However, in more recent times the library has been given printed books of Catholic liturgy which survived the destruction of the Reformation. There is a *Missal* (Sarum Rites) of 1526 printed in Paris. The Missal lays out in Latin the texts for the celebration of the Mass. We have a *Pontificale* of 1561 printed in Venice. A Pontifical is the guidance for a bishop giving sacraments and does not include the text of the Mass. The most interesting is a *Processionale ad usum*

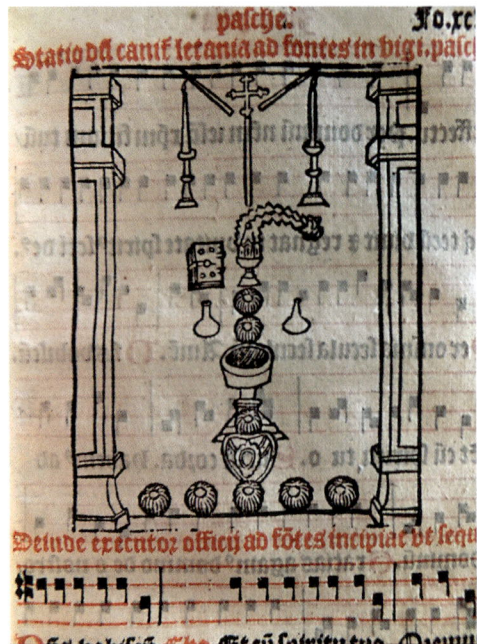

A *Processionale* of 1544

which sets out the music and "choreography" for the services involving processions and has illustrations with tonsured heads indicating who goes where and what they should be carrying. This was printed in London in 1544.

The Scottish BCP caused a riot?

King Charles I resolved at his coronation in Scotland that the Scots should share the Church of England's liturgy rather than the Presbyterian *Book of Common Order* that they had adopted after the Reformation. The non-Presbyterian Scottish bishops amended the 1559 Book of Common Prayer in their draft of a new liturgy and this was approved by Archbishop Laud.

The new *Book of Common Prayer for Scotland* published in Edinburgh in 1637 was rejected as an Anglo-Catholic threat to their chosen Calvinist Protestantism. The first attempt to use it on 23rd July 1637 resulted in a protest in St. Giles' Cathedral, Edinburgh. A market trader called Jenny Geddes threw her stool at the head of the Dean and she and her friends were ejected. Later in the day riots broke out in Edinburgh in support of the protest. A Covenant was signed by those in opposition to

Rioting resulting from use of Scotland's new Book of Common Prayer.

the changes being forced on Scotland and this opposition then led directly to the Bishops' Wars between Scotland and England, fought between 1639 and 1640. The Scottish armies defeated the poorly trained militia of the English, many of the English soldiers having no stomach to fight as they had Puritan beliefs more in accord with the Scots.

The 1637 *Book of Common Prayer* came to be used by the Scottish Episcopal Church. It also influenced the liturgy of the American Episcopal Church as their first bishop was consecrated in Scotland in 1784. The Chained Library has a chained copy of the Scottish BCP.

What is the 1662 Sealed Book?

The 1662 BCP is sometimes referred to as the "sealed book". At the Restoration of Charles II in 1660, a meeting was convened to attempt a reconciliation between the traditional Anglican bishops and the Puritan and Presbyterian factions. This took place in London in 1661 and is known as the Savoy Conference. The meeting attempted to find a revised liturgy acceptable to all sides. Agreement could not be reached.

The 1662 BCP made some 600 minor changes to the 1559 version and was central to the 1662 Act of Uniformity. The Act required all churchmen to observe the rites and ceremonies of the new BCP or to leave the Anglican church. Some 2,000 clergymen felt unable to do so and this caused a split in the church between Anglicans and Nonconformists, still unresolved.

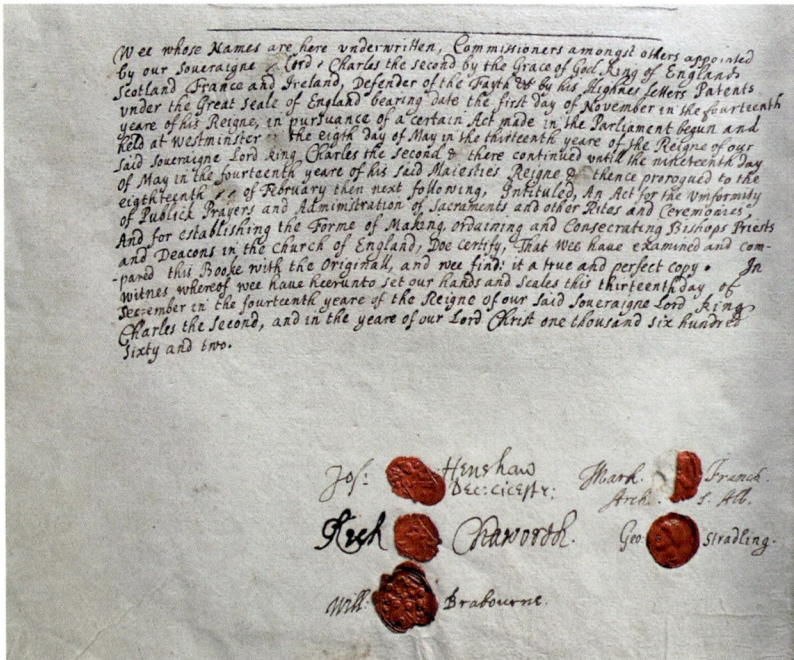

Seal and warrant from the 1662 Book of Common Prayer.

Cathedrals were sent copies of the 1662 BCP. Each copy had a royal warrant from Charles II and was signed by five commissioners with red wax seals to indicate that it was a true copy of the original. There are only twenty-seven such sealed copies thought to have survived and we are very fortunate that we have retained ours.

What happened to the BCP during the Civil War and Commonwealth?

The English Civil War of 1642-46 brought in the government of the country by Parliament which was opposed to the traditional structure of the Church of England, linking it to the values of the Roman Catholic church.

Parliament approved the *Directory for the Publique Worship of God* in 1645 as a replacement for the *Book of Common Prayer*. It is more of an agenda than a fixed liturgy and relies on scripture. Ceremonies and outward gestures such as kneeling were excluded as was singing in the service for burial. This more puritanical form of worship was not popular and many parts of the country did not adopt the *Directory*. Wells cathedral, as all other cathedrals, was closed for fifteen years during the Civil War and Commonwealth. However, we were given a copy of the Directory in 1937.

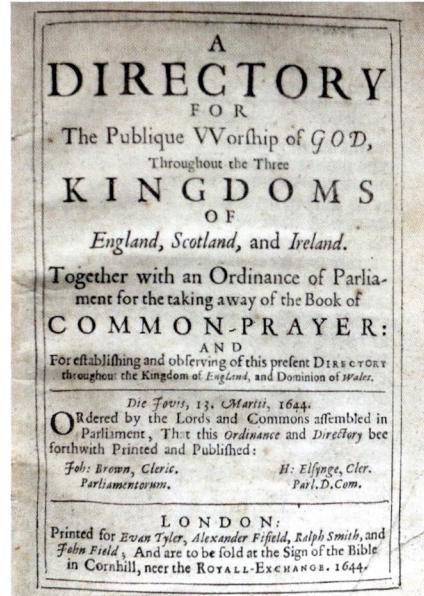

The Civil War Puritan Directory

Do you have the BCP in other languages?

We have a 1621 copy of the BCP in Welsh. The book was translated in 1567 by Humphrey Toy and printed as *Y Llyfr Gweddi Gyffredin*. The Chained Library also has two copies of the BCP in Arabic, both given by Bishop George Hooper (1704-27).

The Bath Abbey collection has a BCP in Latin published in 1670. A Latin translation seems slightly bizarre but was authorised for use in Ireland in 1560. The Irish parliament recognised that English speaking priests were scarce and mainly resided in the Pale around Dublin. To reach the rest of Ireland, a Latin version was authorised, this still being too early for printing in Gaelic.

WHERE CAN I READ MORE ABOUT THIS?

There are facsimile copies of the 1549 BCP and the manuscript of the 1662 BCP (in the Reading Room at 264)

DAILEY, PRUDENCE (ed.) – *The Book of Common Prayer: past, present and future* – Continuum, 2011 (in the Reading Room shelved at 264)

PROCTOR, FRANCIS and FRERE, WALTER – *A New History of the Book of Common Prayer* Macmillan, 1925 (in the Reading Room shelved at 264)

CHAPTER EIGHTEEN

Bookbinding

Are all the books in the Chained Library bound in leather?

ALMOST 100% of the bindings are either leather or parchment, which is untanned animal skin, but there are a few with covers made of board and marbled paper. Until 1800, all bookbindings were produced by hand. The day of the publisher producing mechanised bindings in cloth or buckram all looking the same did not arrive until the nineteenth century.

The most common leather is calf. There are a few books bound in morocco leather, which is goatskin, and a few German books are bound in pigskin. One or two of the early manuscript books have a chemise cover made of deerskin. Limp parchment, which looks crinkly and off-white, was used as cheaper or temporary binding on smaller books; it was an early version of the paperback. The parchment was commonly made from sheepskin.

Chemise binding on the illuminated manuscript Hailes Psalter of 1514.

Were the books bound locally?

We have seen in Chapter Thirteen that many of our books were printed in Europe. Binding, however, tended to be done in the country where the book was purchased. Because of the high costs of transport in earlier times, publishers would export books unbound to save on the expense of carriage as they were heavier and bulkier if already bound. Indeed, in 1534 legislation was passed in England forbidding the import of bound books in an attempt to protect the local bookbinders. Even books printed in London would usually be offered either with a "trade" binding arranged by the bookseller, or were sold unbound in case the purchaser wanted to arrange his own binding in a particular style, often know as "fine" binding. The books in the Chained Library are typically trade bound in styles associated with binders in London, Oxford and Cambridge rather than more locally.

Some of the books have wooden covers?

Books throughout the fifteenth century and until about 1550 would usually have wooden boards covering the front and back of the book. This made some sense as wood was strong and durable and books tended to be large. The wood was typically beech or oak and would be covered in leather. The use of wood died out because the number of printed books being produced was increasing and it was impractical to cut down so many trees. It is uncommon to find wooden boards after 1550 except on some larger books. We have a late example in the large Foxe's *Book of Martyrs* from 1583 which has wooden covers and bosses attached on the outside [*see photo in Chapter Two*]. Pasteboard covers made of layers of grey paper glued together became the replacement for wood. The technique of making pasteboard was introduced from the Middle East.

Why do books have clasps?

Manuscript books made of parchment had clasps on the side to keep the book tightly closed. Parchment can crinkle when it gets damp and clasps were an attempt to keep the pages inside flat. Clasps were usually made of metal, most commonly brass. The custom of binding with one or two clasps continued when printed books made of paper were introduced. It was not necessary, but people had grown used to books with clasps and the custom continued until well into the 1530s.

Sixteenth century binding with brass clasps.

You will see a good number of books in the Chained Library that have two green cloth ties to keep the book tightly closed. The ties are inserted into small holes made in the front and back boards and then tied in a bow over the fore-edge. These replaced the metal clasps by the mid-sixteenth century and were used until about the mid-seventeenth century by which time it was realised that they had no real function.

Parchment binding with green cloth ties.

What is a pastedown?

Pastedowns are a means of strengthening the attachment of the text block, or pages of the book, to its cover. One leaf of an endpaper is sewn to the pages whilst the other half is glued to the inside of the front or back cover. This might not sound glamorous but on early books it can be fascinating. The endpapers

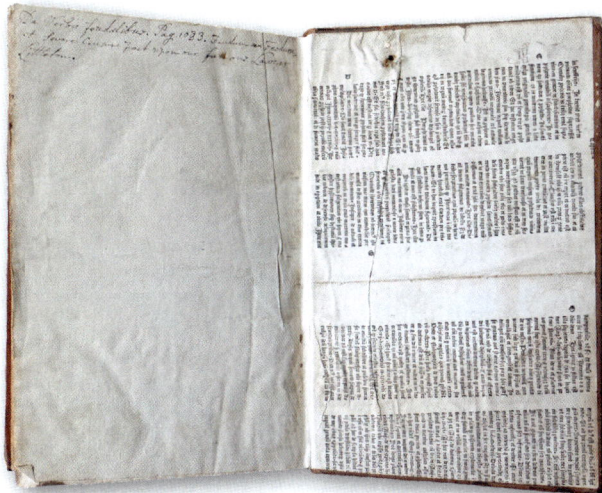

Pastedown on a back board.

used were often scraps of parchment or printer's waste of sheets that had been rejected. Many history of the book specialists examine pastedowns for clues to unknown printed books. In our bound Archive books we have examples of pastedowns that were early music written on parchment and groups have even performed music from them.

Why do some books have spines with ridges?

Binding styles have varied over the years. Continental binders tended to have smooth spines but in England the horizontal raised bands, as they are more properly called, usually four or five in number, are covering the strips of cord or leather that act as sewing supports in the binding process. To achieve a smooth spine, it was sometimes fashionable to cut into the back of the textblock and recess the cords which took over from the leather strips.

Have spines always had lettering?

No. We noted in an earlier chapter that books had originally been laid out flat on lecterns and so the spines were not easily seen. Chained books have the fore-edge outwards with the spines at the back of the shelf, and even unchained books were kept like this until about 1600. It took until 1706 until all the books at Cambridge University library were shelved with their spines outward.

Spine lettering was known in England as early as 1562 but was not common until after 1670. The trade bindings of booksellers were usually unlettered calf throughout the seventeenth century as it cost more to add titles in gilt. Many individuals and institutions then employed someone to apply lettering

Frontispiece of Bishop Brian Walton's Polyglot Bible of 1657, showing books still shelved with their fore-edge outwards.

retrospectively on their books, eg: Durham cathedral library paid 6d a book to have gilt spine letters put on 167 books in 1691.

Can you date a book by the pattern of its binding?

Bookbinding styles evolved over time and you can date books fairly well from their bindings. It must always be borne in mind that books may have been rebound by their owner or new owner to suit a particular style and so not be contemporary, but we look to have few examples of that practice in our collection.

Our earliest manuscript books like the Hailes Psalter will often have DEERSKIN CHEMISES. Books with wooden boards, ie: those from the late fifteenth century to about 1550 may have calf leather, usually dark brown, with patterns on them produced by engraved BRASS ROLLS applied a bit like pastry cutters. These rolls were warmed up and then pressed on the leather to produce the desired pattern. From such books it is quite easy to identify where and roughly when they were bound as the patterns have been documented and classified by scholars such as Basil Oldham.

[*This illustration also shows that Spierinck used the figure* 4 *as a guild mark together with* N *and* S *as the initials of the binder. Use of the figure* 4 *was mentioned in Chapter Eight on Printers' marks.*]

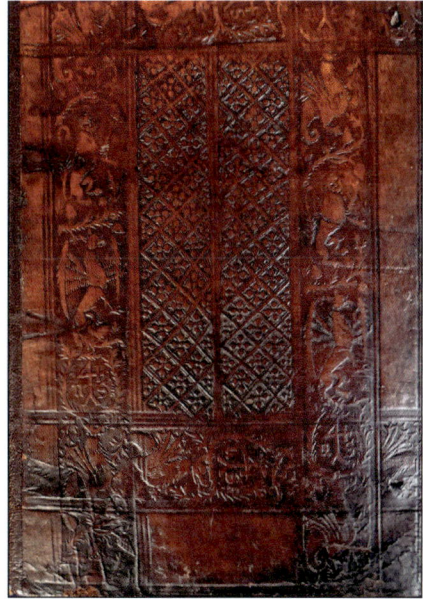

Roll patterns on calf leather binding by Nicolas Spierinck, 1526.

CENTRE-PIECE BINDINGS were common from the 1560s until the 1630s. The centre-pieces are made by pressing an engraved stamp, usually in the shape of an oval or lozenge into the leather. If the design has gold leaf applied it is known as gold tooling; if left without gold or other colouring it is known as blind tooling. This style was introduced from Islamic practice and reached Europe though Venice and the Italian trading ports at the end of the fifteenth century. Throughout this period LIMP PARCHMENT binding could be found on cheaper and smaller books.

PANEL STAMPS were also used from 1570-1630. These tended to be simplified towards the end of the seventeenth century. By this time the calf leather was often lighter and sometimes dilute acid would be sprinkled on the leather to produce patterns that could be called marbled, mottled or speckled.

Centre-piece binding

Gold tooling of panelled fine calf binding on Matthew Prior's *Poems.*

It is worth noting that bookbinding design is invariably abstract rather than pictorial and usually bears no obvious representational relationship with the content of the book. By far the best accessible guide to all of this quite complex subject is David Pearson's well illustrated book *English Bookbinding Styles 1450-1800* which is in the Reading Room shelved at 686.3.

When did marbled paper appear?

Marbled paper was again an Islamic, possibly originally Chinese, invention but it became popular in France in the first quarter of the seventeenth century. It was seen in English books as endpapers as early as the 1630s but was not common until the late seventeenth century. Some of our books, especially those belonging to Bishops Thomas Ken (1685-90) and George Hooper (1704-27) have marbled paper instead of leather on their front and back boards. This was a cheaper expedient and was quite commonly used by students at Oxford.

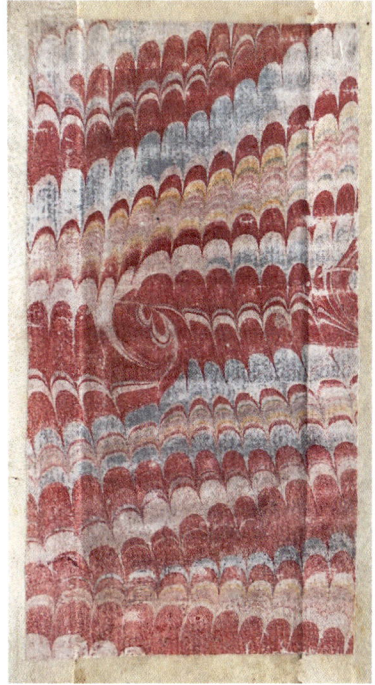

Some of the books have family crests?

Books with a family crest are said to have an armorial binding. We have a sprinkling of such bindings in the library and there is a database at the University of Toronto that has identifying notes on these and all other British armorial bindings: http://armorial.library.utoronto.ca/

The most commonly found in our collection are the books donated by Richard Busby (1606-95) who was the Treasurer of the cathedral and who gave the money for the refurbishing of the library in 1685.

Oxford binding using parchment and marbled paper

far left:
Device of Richard Busby

left:
Coat of Arms of Bishop Creighton (1670-2)

In the Bath Abbey collection are a number of devices belonging to women such as Elizabeth Tufton, Countess of Thanet: [*right*]

Do you have books made by famous bookbinders?
The sad fact is that most bookbinders have remained unrecognised. In the hierarchy of the book trade structure, binders have always been accorded the lowest status and the poorest pay despite their skills. Only librarians fare worse. The best that binders can aspire to is to be known by the patterns found in their work, so we can recognise the "greyhound binder" or the "medallion binder" but no-one knows their name. Even the finest examples of the exquisite Irish bindings of the eighteenth century are only recognised as "parliamentary binder A" or "parliamentary binder B". (Despite its lowly status, book-binding has generated a vast literature about itself. By 1985 there were some 8,000 books and articles recorded in an international bibliography on the subject).

However, in the collection we do have a book bound by Henry VIII's binder, John Reynes, which uses the royal motifs stamped on the leather even though the book was never in the royal collection.

Binding by John Reynes

Another recognised early binder is Nicholas Spierinck (d.1546), who worked in Cambridge, and it is his work that we showed earlier using rolls on leather bound wood.

142

Do you have any fine bindings?

These are not plentiful in the collection. They tend to use coloured morocco leather rather than calf. The goatskin had to be imported and came first from Turkey via Venice in the seventeenth century and then North Africa. As it was not native and had to be imported, it was never common until the late eighteenth century. One good example is the set of the Bible and Book of Common Prayer that belonged to Bishop Robert Creighton (1670-2). This is bound in red morocco with gold tooling. The Bible is one we use when new members of Chapter or clergy have to take an oath in a service downstairs.

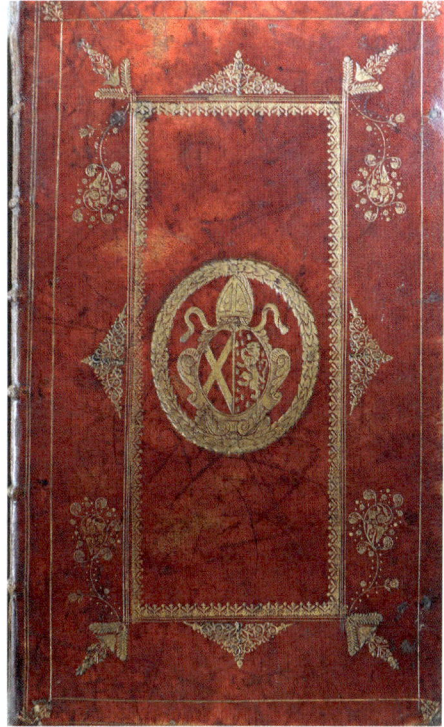

Fine morocco leather on Bishop Creighton's Bible

How much work has to be done to keep the bindings in good condition?

The collection received major investment in conservation during the middle of the last century. Many books were rebacked, ie they kept the original binding on the front and back boards but the worn spines were replaced. For this reason we will never know if the original spine was lettered or not. The rebacking meant that the spines were either lettered for the first time or relettered. The work was not done particularly sympathetically as they have the look of 1950s public library spine letters, some of which even have incorrect spelling. Similarly, many of the original pastedowns were probably lost and replaced with modern paper. But compared with other cathedral libraries, our books are in very good health, lacking the tell-tale brown ribbons tied around the book denoting that the front and back boards have separated.

Every second year we undertake a thorough dusting of the books and shelves and look for signs of damage to the bindings. This is often quite minor but repairs are undertaken by a local bookbinder experienced in working with antiquarian books. At the 2015 dusting we identified forty books needing attention, ie: 1% of the total, and these were mainly front and back boards that were coming loose, or the headbands or tailbands at the top and bottom of the spine were unravelling. The total cost of repairs was under £2,000, which works out to £1,000 a year to maintain the collection. We have fortunately been free of insect or rodent damage, at least in recent years.

WHERE CAN I READ MORE ABOUT THIS?

COCKERELL, DOUGLAS – *Bookbinding and the Care of Books* – Hogg, 1906 (In the Reading Room at 686.3)

FOOT, MIRJAM (ed.) – *Eloquent Witnesses: bookbindings and their witnesses* – British Library, 2004 (In the Reading Room at 095)

OLDHAM, J. BASIL – *Blind Panels of English Binders* – 1958 (In the Reading Room at 686.3)

OLDHAM, J. BASIL – *English Blind-Stamped Bindings* – 1952 (In the Reading Room at 686.3)

PEARSON, DAVID – *English Bookbinding Styles 1450-1800* – British Library, 2005 (In the Reading Room at 686.3)

POLLARD, GRAHAM – *Changes in the Style of Bookbinding, 1550-1830* – The Library, XI, 2, June 1956, pp.71-94

It is also recommended that anyone interested tries to join a tour of the bindery in Bath attached to Bayntun's bookshop. This very traditional workshop still undertakes restoration and fine binding and has tools and equipment that are over 100 years old. The firm itself does not offer tours but it sometimes hosts local societies who wish to visit the bindery.

CHAPTER NINETEEN

Copyright and Censorship

When did copyright begin?

THE FIRST COPYRIGHT ACT in England (and the world) was in 1709, in Queen Anne's reign, and came into force in 1710. The Act was titled "An Act for the Encouragement of Learning, by vesting the Copies of Printed Books in the Authors or purchasers of such Copies, during the Times therein mentioned". This was the first time copyright was awarded to the author rather than giving privileges to the publisher. The period of copyright was for fourteen years with a further extension of fourteen years if the author was still alive. After the author's copyright period ended, the book entered the public domain and other printers could then make copies without fear of penalty. Today's copyright is for the author's lifetime plus seventy years.

What protection for books existed before then?

In the sixteenth century and seventeenth century, there was a close relationship between censorship and what was effectively copyright, even though the term did not exist at that time. Although civil and religious authorities had welcomed the invention of printing, they were also aware of its dangers. The Tudor state did not feel it had the ability to control every possible printing press and so it set up, by royal charter, the incorporation of the Stationers' Company in London in 1557 to do the job for it. The trade-off was simple: the Stationers were given the printing monopoly in England provided that they ensured no heretical material or books critical of the civil authorities were printed. Only twenty-one printers were authorised in London using fifty-three printing presses, all of these printers having to be members of the Stationers' Company, and only Oxford and Cambridge universities were allowed to print books outside London. With the exception of allowing printing in York from 1662, this situation continued virtually unchanged until 1695. By European standards, these restrictions on printing were unparalleled.

The Stationers' Company maintained a Register and every authorised book was recorded so that the printer was known. During various periods from 1557 to 1695, books had to be licensed before printing. For

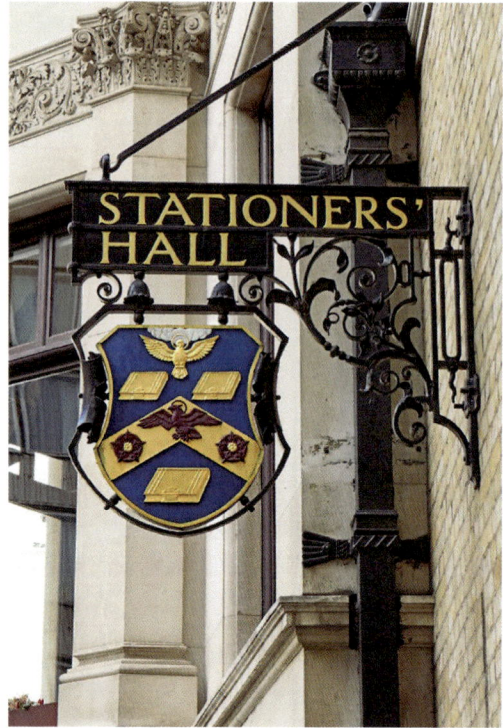

Stationers' Hall coat of arms

much of the time it was the Archbishop of Canterbury, the Bishop of London or the Lord Chancellor who had the power to approve or license a book for printing. They in turn would delegate the power to chaplains or subject specialists. Certain books were exempt as they were given a royal privilege which printers had to purchase. This amounted to a monopoly so that a particular printer or group of printers had exclusive rights to print Bibles, law books, Latin primers, almanacs, etc. and it was a punishable offence for any other printer to produce a book covered by the royal privilege or warrant.

From the printers point of view, once their book was on the Register, they had the sole rights in perpetuity to print that book. They could, however, sell the rights to another printer, or printers, if they wished. This gave them protection from book piracy whereby another printer could make an unauthorised copy of their work and, by selling it, reduce their profits. The Stationers' Company had considerable powers of search, confiscation and imprisonment should they receive complaints of piracy or even unauthorised printing presses.

Effectively, this was a form of early copyright but it was given to the publisher and not the author of the work, unlike the 1709 Act. And trade copyright worked well: book piracy was uncommon; there were enough members of the Company to allow competition; books were reasonably priced; authors were paid; journeymen in the printing houses were not noticeably worse off than in other trades.

Were all books placed on the Register?

No. It is estimated that in the early days a third were not registered so that control was not complete. A printer had to pay 6d to register a book and it was only worth their while if they thought that someone might pirate the book. Ephemeral or very local material was often not registered. However, the injunctions of the Star Chamber in 1586, which desired all printed material to be registered encouraged more entries, and the Star Chamber decree of 1637 led to an even higher rate of registration giving the government more surveillance and control. Pressure from the Stationers' Company to ensure no publication escaped licensing elicited John Milton's *Areopagitica* in 1644. It is still one of the most eloquent pleas for defence of intellectual liberty and freedom of expression even though it had little effect in its day.

Foreign imported books were a large part of the book trade at this time as printing was cheaper and better on the continent. However, book imports could only be made into London ports and all books were taken from the docks to the Stationers' Hall to be examined before sale was permitted.

What led to the Copyright Act of 1709?

During the Civil War of the 1640s and the ensuing Commonwealth period, normal regulations regarding the press were abandoned. Charles II restored these with the 1662 Licensing Act for *"preventing the frequent Abuses in printing seditious treasonable and unlicensed Bookes and Pamphlets and for regulating Printing and Printing Presses"*. However, by this time with Protestantism well established, censorship was more to protect the government than the church.

This Act also gave recognition to trade copyright in legal terms for the first time:

No person or persons shall hereafter print or cause to be imprinted nor shall forge put or counterfeit in or upon any Booke or Pamphlet the Name Marke Title or Vinnet of any other person or persons which hath or shall have lawfull Priviledge Authority or Allowance of sole printing the same, without the free consent of the person or persons so priviledged first had and obtained.

The 1662 Act effectively restored the monopoly of the Stationers' Company. Sir Roger L'Estrange was made the Surveyor of the Imprimery and Licenser of the Press and was zealous in carrying out his suppression of heretical or treasonable publications. Many books in the Chained Library bear his name showing that they were licensed for printing.

Eventually, however, the freedoms expressed in the Bill of Rights of 1689 led to more resentment of the powers of the Stationers' Company, especially the length of a book's privilege being in perpetuity. By 1694 the government refused to renew the law which granted them their monopoly. The

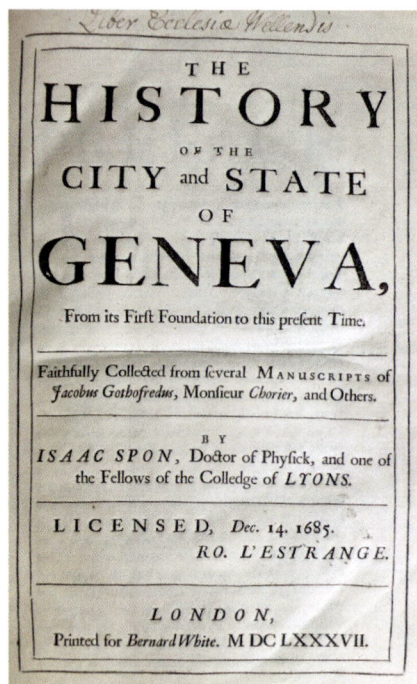

Book licensed by Roger L'Estrange in 1685.

lapse of the Licensing Law in 1695 led to a growth in printing presses and publishing throughout the country. The Stationers were very resentful of the loss of their privileges and mounted many pleas and protests. At the same time, authors such as Jonathan Swift and Daniel Defoe were also demanding copyright protection for their writing as the lapse of the Licensing Act meant there was none. Eventually, the Stationers worked out that a new law giving copyright to authors could work to their advantage as authors had little choice but to assign their copyright to the publishers.

148

Did we not have books burned in earlier times?

The earliest form of censorship in England was religious censorship. Books such as the Wyclif Bible in English, produced in manuscript in the 1380s, were declared heretical. Henry IV's law of 1401, *De Heretico Comburendo*, forbade anyone to read or own a copy of the Bible in English on pain of being burnt to death. But this was before printing which posed a much greater threat. Cardinal Wolsey decreed on 14 May 1521 that all books by the heretic Martin Luther were to be surrendered and burnt. Later, copies of Tyndale's printed Bible in English were publicly burned in London on repeated occasions, much encouraged by Sir Thomas More and Cuthbert Tunstall who was the Bishop of London. Distributing copies of Tyndale's Bible could lead to an individual being burnt at the stake, a fate that befell Richard Bayfield.

The Roman Catholic Church also had a list of banned books?

The Catholic Church set up the *Index Librorum Prohibitorum et Expurgatorium* in 1559 in response to the Protestant Reformation. This was a list of books that its adherents were banned from reading as they were deemed to be immoral or contained theological errors. The list was continually added to and only abolished in 1966, by which time the works of Graham Greene and D. H. Lawrence were on it. The list was largely post publication. The Catholic Church tried to prevent publication of books it did not approve of and was largely successful through the Inquisition in countries recognising its jurisdiction. But the book trade was fairly global and books were widely exported, so it was necessary to condemn books acquired from elsewhere.

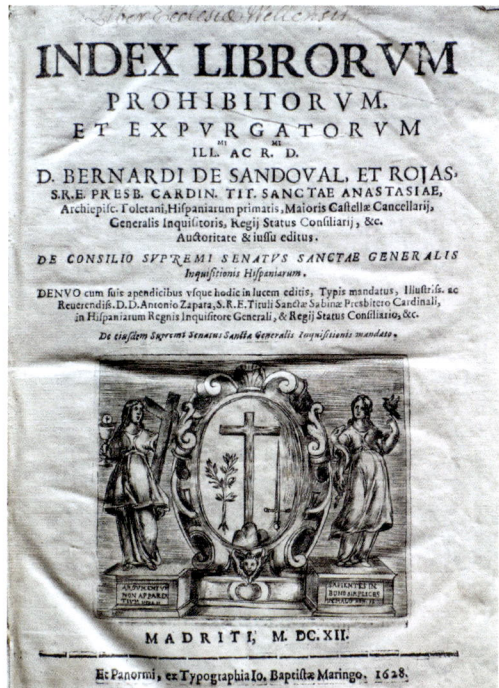

[*right*] The Chained Library has a copy of the 1612 list printed in Spain.

The larger part of the list was the *Expurgatorium* whereby someone could own or read a particular book provided certain passages were removed or made illegible. Many works by Erasmus, Polydore Vergil, William Camden and others were included in this section.

Are these days of censorship and book destruction behind us in the present day?

Far from it. Most people are aware of the book burnings by the Nazis, and of the illicit circulation of samizdat books in manuscript in the Soviet Union where the books were banned and could not be printed and circulated, eg: Pasternak and Solzshenitsyn. But in England, the unexpurgated version of D. H. Lawrence's *Lady Chatterley's Lover* faced trial under the Obscene Publications Act in 1960, and in the 1980s the government tried to ban the ex-MI5 agent Peter Wright's book *Spycatcher*. Even today, possession of the *Anarchist Cookbook* could see you prosecuted under the Terrorism Act of 2000.

On a much larger scale we have witnessed the deliberate destruction of two million books in the Bosnian National Library by the Bosnian Serbs in the war of 1992. This led to a very brave librarian called Mustafa Jahic evacuating all the 10,000 items in his 500 hundred year old library of Oriental material in the Gazi Husrev Bey Library to spare them similar destruction. Books were smuggled out at night under sniper fire in banana crates for refuge in safe houses and to be microfilmed in case of destruction. They included a manuscript by an Islamic scientist dated to 1106. The manuscripts have now been restored to a new building opened in Sarajevo in 2014.

Mustafa Jahic *(Photo courtesy of https://gerryco23.wordpress.com/2012/09/21/the-love-of-books-a-sarajevo-story/)*

Another hero worth celebrating is Abdel Kader Haidara. He smuggled out Islamic manuscripts from Timbuktu after Al-Qaeda in the Islamic Maghreb took over the city in 2012 and started burning them. The mostly scientific manuscripts dated from the thirteenth century to the seventeenth century. Haidara organised for the 300,000 manuscripts to be put in metal trunks and loaded on donkey carts and then boats to be smuggled out of Timbuktu through jihadist checkpoints. They were taken to

Abdel Kader Haidara *(photo courtesy of http://news.nationalgeographic. com/news/innovators/2014/04/140421-haidara-timbuktu-manuscripts-mali- library-conservation/)*

the relative safety of the Malian capital of Bamako in the south.

It is interesting that at Wells cathedral we have preserved the cathedral's archives fairly intact with the earliest item dating back to AD 958. Archive documents are not controversial as they are working documents relating to financial transactions and cathedral events and procedures. Books, however, contain ideas and opinions and will always appear threatening to certain groups of people with contrary ideas. For this reason, we lost our early library at the time of the Reformation and so have only one book left that was at Wells before 1540, the beautiful Pliny *Historia Naturalis*, 1472 that was recovered from an Oxford bookshop by Dean Ralph Bathurst in 1682.

WHERE CAN I READ MORE ABOUT THIS?

BAKER, KENNETH – *On the Burning of Books* – Unicorn, 2016

GLEASON, JOHN – *The earliest evidence for ecclesiastical censorship of printed books in England* – Library, June 1982 pp.135-141

HOTCHKISS, VALERIE and ROBINSON, FRED – *English in Print* – University of Illinois Press, 2008

JOHNS, ADRIAN – *The Nature of the Book* – University of Chicago Press, 1998

POLASTRON, LUCIEN – *Books on Fire* – Inner Traditions, 2004

POLLARD, ALFRED – *Some notes on the history of copyright in England, 1662-1775* – Library, June 1922, pp.97-114

❧ ❧ ❧

General Index

NUMBERS IN RED INDICATE ILLUSTRATION PAGES

❧